The Economics of Small Firms

MAINSTREAM SERIES

GRAHAM BANNOCK

The Economics of Small Firms

Return from the Wilderness

BASIL BLACKWELL · OXFORD

First published in 1981 by
Basil Blackwell Publisher
108 Cowley Road
Oxford OX4 1JF
England

British Library Cataloguing in Publication Data

Bannock, Graham
 The economics of small firms. — (Mainstream).
 1. Small business — Great Britain
 I. Title II. Series
 338.6'42'0941 HD2346.G7

ISBN 0-631-11391-6

Typesetting by Getset, Eynsham
Printed in Great Britain by Billing and Sons Ltd
Guildford, London, Oxford, Worcester

CONTENTS

INTRODUCTION

A person is not likely to be a good economist who is nothing else. Social phenomena acting and reacting on one another, they cannot rightly be understood apart; but this by no means proves that the material and industrial phenomena of society are not themselves susceptible of useful generalisations, but only that these generalisations must necessarily be relative to a given form of civilisation and a given stage of social advancement.

Mill, *On Comte*, quoted by Alfred Marshall in his *Principles of Economics* (1890)

This book is the last of an unplanned trilogy on the theme that the concentration and centralization of our economic institutions is bad for economic and social welfare. *The Juggernauts* (1971) dealt with giant firms. *How to Survive the Slump* (1975) attempted to show how the errors of centralization had led to what I foresaw as a lengthy recession. This book on small firms proposes a way forward.

It might be said that in writing on this subject I am now pushing at an open door. But much of contemporary discussion seems to me to be very superficial and the action taken so far falls far short of what is necessary. Perhaps I should emphasize here, as I have in the text, that promoting small business is not an immediate panacea for all our economic problems. Nor, as I hint at several points in the book, is monetarism (even with the two-year lag its proponents sensibly insist upon), or any other macro-economic approach. To restrict the growth of the money supply within the limits of real output growth is one prerequisite for the control of inflation and the restoration of economic health, but much else is necessary. Some economists talk about the economy as if it were some great fruit machine and that restless manipulation of interest rates, exchange rates, subsidies, import controls or some other variable will one day hit the combination that releases the jackpot. There are no instant solutions: the pursuit of bigness is one of the manifestations of a greed for quick, easy results and its failure has demonstrated its fruitlessness.

The theme of this book is that there is now an overwhelming presumption that the evident ills of the economic system and the decline of small business have common roots and that action to stimulate small business will have beneficial effects upon the economy as a whole. In chapter 7 I have sketched out some of the things which might be done, or rather the direction that action should take. This is not a complete programme; I have tried to show that the whole of our economic and social system (not merely in Britain but in all the advanced market economies) has been channelling effort and resources away from small business and much more research is required before we can understand the nature of the forces at work and prescribe comprehensive remedies. What is clear is that powerful vested interests will resist change. It will be argued, for this reason, that some of the proposals made are politically unrealistic. In fact, under the pressure of events, political realities can and do change remarkably quickly and it is hoped that in some small way this book will contribute to that process.

Research on small firms and their role in economic development is in its infancy, but I have tried to summarize what is known and the direction in which *I think* present knowledge is pointing. I have striven to write briefly and in simple language. In keeping with this aim I have included two interludes. The first of these (chapter 2) can be skipped by readers with practical experience in small business. The second (chapter 5), which attempts to communicate the complexity of the debate among economists on the macro-economic issues which form the backdrop of the book, can be passed by professionals who will find it unrepresentative of all shades of opinion.

I have kept statistics and references to a minimum and the short bibliography gives a very inadequate indication of my debts to other authors. I have also benefited much from participation in research programmes financed by Shell UK Ltd, the Anglo German Foundation, the European Commission, the Association of Independent Business and the British Forum of Private Business. Finally, I should like to thank Alan Peacock who prompted me to write the book, Ron Baxter and Peter Cropper who read and commented on parts of the first draft and Stan Mendham to whom I owe the germ of the idea of comprehensive 'package' legislation for small firms which is put forward in chapter 7.

Graham Bannock

March, 1980

CHAPTER 1

The New Economic Environment

The Decline of Small Business

Small firms are owner-managed businesses of modest scale. The term is not unambiguous and we shall need to define it more precisely later. However defined, the share of small firms in the total economic activity has declined drastically in the twentieth century. Whilst it remains true that of all independent enterprises the vast majority are small (94 per cent of enterprises in UK manufacturing employ 200 persons or less) their share in employment and output has fallen. In 1935 these small manufacturing firms accounted for 38 per cent of employment, by 1968 their share had fallen to 19 per cent and the number of such firms had fallen even faster, from 136,000 to 58,000, that is to say the average size of 'small' firms had increased. The share of small firms in employment has also declined in most other sectors of the economy and particularly rapidly in retailing.

The decline in the economic weight of small firms has been reflected in a major shift in the proportion of the working population that earns its income from profits as distinct from wages or salaries. In 1911, according to the censuses of population, 25.5 per cent of the labour force consisted of employers and the self-employed. By the early 1970s this proportion had fallen to around 7.5 per cent.

The counterpart of the decline of small firms has been the growing importance of a small number of giant companies. According to S. J. Prais (1976), the share of the hundred largest enterprises in UK net output rose from 16 per cent in 1909 to around 40 per cent in 1970.

Another major change which, as we shall see, is intimately connected with the decline of small firms, has been the increased role of the State in the economy. Central and local government expenditure as a proportion of the Gross National Product (GNP) rose from about 9 per cent in 1890 to nearly 50 per cent in the middle 1970s, and the public sector, including the nationalized industries, now employs well over a quarter of the UK working population.

Whereas, at the beginning of this century the majority of the population in Britain worked in small firms, the majority now works for large firms or the government. This dramatic change has not been confined to Britain; the rise of the State and large companies and the decline of small firms seems to be common to all the advanced countries, although the pace of change has varied and seems to have gone further in Britain than elsewhere.

Until the middle 1970s, it was generally assumed that the decline of small business was an inevitable, and indeed necessary condition of economic modernization and growth. In the 1960s, in particular, the main thrust of government industrial policy was to stimulate mergers and concentration and there was a flood of books and articles on the subject. Servan Schreiber's *The American Challenge* (1968), for example, urged that the European countries should concentrate their industrial companies into larger units to avert the threat of domination by US multinationals. Many economists, particularly in the US, expressed concern at the effects upon competition of continued concentration, but there were technical difficulties in measuring this adequately and the majority were eager to hasten the decline of the small firm. Just as the horse drawn plough had given way to the tractor, so too were large and increasingly multinational companies taking over the bulk of economic activity in the advanced countries. J. K. Galbraith (1967) wrote, 'By all but the pathologically romantic, it is now recognised that this is not the age of the small man.'

The 1974 Recession and the Ensuing Reappraisal

Towards the end of the 1960s, evidence of the increase in concentration that had taken place since the end of World War II began to accumulate and concern began to mount about the persistence of the inflationary pressures that accompanied the growth of the world economy. In 1973-74, following the quadrupling of oil prices by OPEC, this growth stopped abruptly. Although the actual decline in output in all the industrialized countries was very mild by the standards of the inter-war slump, it was none the less traumatic. The post-war period had seen virtually uninterrupted growth for 30 years. Real Gross Domestic Product (GDP) per head in the developed market economies had grown at an annual average compound rate of about 3.9 per cent per annum between 1950 and 1970. Since 1970 the average has been about 2.5 per cent. There was a standstill in growth between 1973 and 1975, (with absolute declines in some countries, the largest being a 9.5 per cent fall in the US); thereafter growth has recovered at a slower rate, but a further recession is now generally expected for 1980-81 following further increases in the price of oil. Unemployment in the 1960s averaged less than 3 per cent and early in 1980 was over 5 per cent (nearly 17 million people in the member countries of the OECD).

There is now a growing realization that a resumption of rapid economic growth could be deferred for some time yet and that the 1973-74 recession marks a definite break in the post-war era of prosperity. The conventional wisdom is that the increase in oil prices is largely responsible for two reasons: first because it transfers real income from oil consumers in the advanced countries to the developing economies of the oil producers who cannot immediately spend their increased income on imported goods and services; second and more importantly because increased energy costs have given another upward twist to the inflationary spiral. Although output is increasing only slowly and although there is unemployment among both men and machines, governments cannot stimulate demand for fear of pushing inflation still higher.

It is important to put the role of increased oil prices into perspective: they are only one element in a much deeper problem and should not be confused with the real causes of inflation and recession. There were clear signs of a slowing down in the rate of capital formation in the 1960s and early 1970s. The rate of increase in prices was also increasing long before the 1973-74 oil crisis. For example in Britain, on average, the retail price index rose by 2.7 per cent a year between 1960 and 1964, by 4.3 per cent between 1965 and 1969, and by 12.1 per cent between 1970 and 1974. The development of increasing domestic oil production in the UK has not prevented Britain from suffering more than most other countries from inflation. Clearly other forces are at work.

Inflation, Causes and Remedies

Various explanations are given of the increased vulnerability of the world economy to inflation. Some economists see it as the consequence of a world-wide tendency by governments to allow the money supply to grow too fast. This is the monetarist point of view which now seems to prevail, certainly in Britain. Others see it as the result of the growth of trade union power in pushing up wages faster than output, a process to which the growth of monopoly power in both the private and public sectors of industry has contributed. This might be called the neo-Keynesian view.

These two points of view are not necessarily inconsistent, since any general increase in prices requires an increase in the quantity of money relative to the quantity of goods and services being produced. The dispute is mainly about whether or not increases in money supply actually *cause* increases in prices or whether they have simply been necessary to finance increases in wages and prices. It is in prescribing a cure that the distinction becomes important. If the monopoly power of unions, large companies and State industry is the first cause of inflation then the answer is to control prices and incomes. If it is a too rapid increase in the money supply, then the answer is to restrain the growth of the quantity of money by cutting back on the growth of public expenditure, controlling bank deposits and raising interest rates.

Both sets of remedies have been tried though their respective adherents would claim that there has not been sufficient persistence. Prices and incomes policies were in force in Britain almost continuously from 1965 until 1979 when they were abandoned by the new Conservative Government. The preceding Labour Government at times also applied quite severe restrictions upon the growth of the money supply and the Conservatives have continued and indeed intensified this policy. A fair and full discussion of the history of anti-inflation policies lies outside the scope of this book. Neither prices and incomes nor monetarist policies has been pursued comprehensively enough or long enough for there to be any certainty about the consequences. In theory, either policy should work at least for a time. Within the limits imposed by the speed with which money circulates, prices cannot rise when the quantity of money is fixed unless output declines. Even then inflation will eventually be checked as some producers will be forced to reduce prices in order to sell anything, and wages must fall if unemployment is not to increase indefinitely. By definition, if prices and incomes are controlled tightly enough they cannot increase.

Each set of policies has its unpleasant and, in contemporary circumstances, possibly self-defeating consequences. Although we cannot be sure, it seems highly likely that, if pursued persistently, even the gradual reduction in the growth of the money supply under the inflationary conditions that have been experienced recently would lead to bankruptcies and growing unemployment. The induced slump would reverse itself in time as inflation was shaken out of the system, but it remains to be seen whether, in a democratic society, any government would have the nerve or the power to push things that far. It is important to emphasize that no post-war government has permanently pushed down high rates of inflation in this way, at least as a result of preconceived policy, so that any government that attempts to do so is, as it were, working in the dark.

Prices and incomes policies certainly do work in the short run, but their history is that pressures build up like steam under a kettle lid which eventually means that controls have to be relaxed and as soon as they are relaxed, prices start rising again. Prices rise because too much money is chasing too few goods. Since the cure for inflation must therefore involve the readjustment of output in relation to demand and since the freezing of prices and incomes tends to reduce the ability of the economy to adapt (because in the market economy relative changes in prices and incomes are the means by which resources are directed to where they are needed) it is difficult to see how price and income control can be anything other than self-defeating.

What underly these dilemmas are the massive changes

that have taken place in the structure of the economic and social system during this century and which were mentioned earlier. The growth of the public sector has been associated with an increase in the pressure of demand upon available resources and a tendency for the money supply to increase faster than output. The growth of concentration in the private sector has enhanced the power of companies to pass on price increases and of unions to push up wages. Both these elements have been reinforced by social changes, increased education for example, which have increased the aspirations and demands of the population. These social changes, for example an insistence upon security which manifests itself in demands that jobs must not be threatened by economic change, contrast with a desire for more equality and more social expenditure that increase demands upon an economic system, a system which must change if these demands are to be met. Inflation seems, in effect, an inevitable product of modern society and has now brought the prospect of continued economic growth into question.

The Relevance of Small Firms

In the years to come, continued restraint in the growth of the money supply in relation to output will be necessary in all the market economies and it seems possible that recourse will again be had to controls on prices and incomes of some sort. This is not as simple as it appears. Like so much else in economics the money supply is not easily defined or, in practice, measured, and there are domestic institutional limitations on the government's ability to control it. To complicate matters still further the money supply and inflation are influenced by developments outside the country. Inflation free growth will not be resumed until quite massive structural and institutional changes have taken place.

Indeed, from another point of view (economic affairs are too complicated to be understood from only one viewpoint) the problems of Western economies are the result of a failure to adjust to changed conditions of demand, technology and relative costs. The post-war boom was so continuous and the pressure of demand so great that once the long-term increase in the rate of inflation was halted in 1974 as it had to be sooner or later if it was not be become explosive, then all kinds of firms and activities which had been sustained only by continuously increasing rates of inflation were suddenly exposed to the chill wind of severe contraction. Shipbuilding, aeronautics, textiles, steel, passenger car and parts of the engineering industries are examples. Vast resources of men and capital are tied up in these industries whilst in others, such as electronics, some services and other parts of engineering, there are chronic shortages of skilled labour. Even so, many large firms which wish to expand and have the financial resources to do so complain that there is a lack of profitable investment opportunities open to them.

Paradoxically this complaint is not often heard from small firms. Many surveys show that a large proportion of these firms cannot get the labour, or the premises or the capital to exploit the markets open to them, in other words small firms are restricted by lack of resources, large firms by demand. That this is so shows that market forces are being impeded and resources are not flowing to the areas where they are needed: large firms can get the resources but in general cannot find sufficient profitable uses for them; small firms can find the opportunities but not the resources.

The principal economic importance of small firms lies in their responsiveness to change and since change is what is required if economic growth is to be resumed, it is desirable that more rather than fewer resources should be channelled into small businesses. Being small and individually owned and managed by fewer people they are more flexible than large firms. Since they have limited resources and are at the mercy of market forces, they have no option but to change when conditions change if they are to survive at all. Many do not survive: American experience suggests that three-quarters of new small firms fail within a few years and the annual death rate for the whole small firm population in the UK is probably over 5 per cent. The failure of a single small firm, or for that matter the starting up of a new one, has no measurable effect upon the economy, however, and no political repercussions; it is part of the seamless band of economic change. Very large firms can rarely be allowed to fail suddenly: the collapse of British Leyland would directly throw over 150,000 people out of work and would have major repercussions on its supplying industries and retailers. It is true that large firms can and do diversify into new activities, but these diversifications usually involve the acquisition of existing companies and, except in those few industries from which small firms are completely excluded by scale or capital requirements, they normally move in directions pioneered by small firms. Small firms, therefore, and especially new small firms, are the prime initiators of new industries and new markets. As new firms start up and others fail they are testing out new products, processes and forms of organization without committing large amounts of resources and without causing disruption if they fail. Of course large firms innovate too and in some fields the requirements of capital and organization require scale, but most large firms started off as small and many if not most innovations were not and probably could not have been initiated from the outset by a large organization. Since what we now lack are new industries to replace the declining ones we cannot afford to neglect what historically has been the foundation of most economic activity. It is very striking that at the beginning of the 1970s when the fashion for bigness was at its peak, concern was being expressed about the long-term socially disruptive effects of the increasing flow of innovation (as for example, in Alvin Toffler's book *Future Shock*) now we bemoan the lack of it. President Carter, who in 1979 set up a taskforce on the problem of innovation, did so in a very different spirit from President Kennedy who in 1961 decided to send America to the moon.

There are other reasons besides innovation for thinking that small firms are relevant to contemporary problems. Small firms, because they lack market power, cannot contribute to inflation: they are price takers not price makers. As decentralized and labour intensive units of production they impose fewer demands upon scarce energy resources or upon the social infrastructure. Labour relations are less of a problem in small firms than large and when individually they run into difficulties there are less painful consequences for the rest of society. In a wider sense an economy consisting largely of small firms has a broader dispersion of economic power than one in which output and employment is concentrated in a small number of large units. Small firms also play a vital role in the economic and social fabric of both rural areas and cities.

The recent upsurge of international interest in small firms owes much to the spread of the idea that small firms are labour intensive and hence that to promote them will do much to mitigate the unemployment problem. Although this idea is, in fact, soundly based, this book tries to show that the problem of small firms has the same roots as our other economic problems. This does not mean that small firms are a panacea, but simply that in dealing with some of the systematic features of modern society which account for the decline in the role of small firms, we shall be contributing to the solution of the economic problem as a whole.

CHAPTER 2

Interlude: a Day in the Life of a Small Firm Proprietor

John Heslop pattered down the damp stairway at the back of the restaurant which led onto the rear garage yard from the flat above, the black iron frame shaking as he went. The cold morning air was a bit of a shock and half way down, with his feet slipping, he realized he should have gone more slowly, but he had hold of the cold rail each side. Only five years ago he would probably have jumped the last three steps, but he was 48 next month and increasingly aware that HESLOP MOTORS LTD would be in serious trouble if he was off work for very long. It was not just the garage, but the restaurant they had added to it five years ago, and the trailer business that was just about ready to get off the ground (or was it?). He was a big man with a shock of black hair, an old oil-stained blazer with leather around the cuffs. His fingers on the rail were nicotine-stained.

John had started in business on his own ten years ago after being made redundant by Laidlows, the coachbuilders on the other side of town. When the firm had been taken over by a larger group, Busbodies United, the new owners had closed the maintenance shop which he managed because they wanted to sell the site for redevelopment. He had been offered the assistant managership of the group main workshop, but he could see that that would never work as soon as he met the manager, a rather smooth young man not too long out of technical college, whose attitude had been distinctly patronizing. John had never taken any exams but had served an apprenticeship with a heavy diesel engine manufacturer and had two years with REME at the end of the war. He was never very good at getting on with 'theoreticians'. This was why he had stuck it out with Laidlows for so long. Old Mr William Laidlow was a practical man himself and had a soft spot for him. Somehow Mr William had persuaded Busbodies to make John redundant and thus pay him redundancy money, which they need not have done since he had been offered another job.

Estate duty was the immediate reason why Laidlows had accepted the bid from Busbodies. Mr William's brother had died suddenly and the coach building market had been rather depressed at the time (it was booming now). The brothers had never bothered to set up a trust that would protect their estate in the event of their death, but ways could have been found round that if William had really cared. They owned property all over the seaside town and their credit was good. But Mr Laidlow was getting tired of it all and neither brother had provided for any proper management succession and there were no sons to take over.

Mr Laidlow had given John advice and some help in setting up on his own. The advice was mainly cautionary: 'It's *always* hard setting up on your own and it's a sad fact that most people fail. It's probably harder now than it's ever been: I couldn't do now what I did 50 years ago.' But the help as usual was practical. The oil company which Laidlows had dealt with for many years, and for which they had at one time maintained tankers, had a service station for lease on the outskirts of town on the coast road and John had been accepted as a tenant on the Laidlow recommendation. The station was well located and equipped, but there was no money in selling petrol.

John's redundancy money had been enough to provide working capital (the bank was not willing to lend very much unsecured to someone without a track record) but they had to keep open at all hours to make it pay. In those days his wife Margaret helped out on the pumps and it was no fun in the winter. The servicing business built up only very slowly and after a couple of years John took on an imported car dealership which, after the initial teething troubles, made a lot of difference. Overheads had risen sharply: he had to find over £20,000 for special equipment, stock and demonstration models alone, (it would be over £50,000 today) as well as take on another mechanic and a part-time salesman. More money was needed to fit out the showroom and for working capital. What had made it possible was a £15,000 legacy when Margaret's father died. With a bank loan, that had just been enough. He had been so short of working capital that he had to push out almost all his trade-ins to other dealers always at considerably less than he allowed the customer for them. He just could not afford the capital to have a stock of used cars on the forecourt. For two years it was touch and go. There was no question of holidays, or for that matter weekends off; it was a seven-day week. They had trouble in holding good mechanics and John had to do quite a lot of the trickier work himself.

But he had been fortunate in his choice of make; in some years he could not get all the cars that he could sell and he now had a good full-time salesman and a service manager. His daughter Jane at 18 was looking after the books. From 1974 onwards things took a turn for the worse again. The business was still viable, but it was up and down and he did not really seem to be getting anywhere. The petrol sales were now self-service, the oil company had paid for the re-equipment but the rent was higher and he was not much better off. The bank were now willing to see him through the bad times but he did not feel that the business was on a really sound footing yet; he was not building up reserves as he should have been and he was already getting bored with the routine. It was in 1974 that the vacant site next to the filling station had come up for sale. They decided to sell their house and buy the land and convert one of the two buildings on it into a restaurant with a flat above.

This was a tremendous risk, but Margaret, whose parents had run a small hotel, had always wanted to run a restaurant and since the children were grown up this was a perfect opportunity to do it. Financing had again been a problem; no Building Society would make an advance on the flat (it was not purpose-built and anyway the building was too old and besides that they did not lend on commercial property). But the bank helped them out again, they did not need very much because they had received a good price for their house and the site had been cheap. It would have been more 'tax efficient' to borrow for the flat, as Bob their accountant said, but they did not really have any choice.

Of course they had grossly underestimated the problem of equipping and running the restaurant and it had taken them time to collect the necessary reliable staff. But Margaret was an outstanding cook and from the start had kept to small menus based on local fish and produce and had the nerve to price fully in line with the quality she was providing. They had managed to get a full on-licence and some help and financial assistance from a local brewer. The clientele built up quickly and now, four years after they had decided to go ahead with it, the restaurant was making nearly as much as the garage, a lot steadier and with fewer problems. It also needed less capital and they had paid off quite a lot of the bank term loan on the property. Unfortunately, inflation had pushed up the working capital needs of the garage substantially and the bank overdraft was now pretty big.

John walked across the yard and into the back of the showroom where his office was. The glass panelled door stuck at the bottom and needed a good push to open it. He would have to see to that and the whole place could do with a repaint inside and out. It was five years since it had been done but he could not see himself finding £2,000 or more for that this year. The mail was on his desk and through the window he could see the salesman working on some finance house paperwork for a new car they had sold yesterday. His daughter, Jane, was sitting at the cash desk, telling a customer through the microphone to press the red button on the pump. Sally, the cashier, was having a baby and would be away for months yet. He could not replace her because she had told him that she intended to demand her job back. Had she been good he would have offered it to her anyway, but she was not good and the Employment Protection Act would not allow him to get someone better if she did not want to leave. With Jane spending most of her time at the cash desk, he could not get her to do the figures he had hoped to show Bob, his accountant, today. Looking over his shoulder through the back window he could see into the workshop across the yard. The roof lights threw their harsh light onto the yellow electronic diagnostic unit, the wheel balancer and the car lift and the long bench with the tools clipped on the wall. The two mechanics in blue overalls were in the corner and he could see that Mr Jones' car was not ready yet. He would be in at 9.30 and there would be hell to pay.

John got up and ran across the yard. On the way he noticed the outside light was on and switched it off: funny how you could never get the staff to remember that. No wonder he was still the same weight as he had been twenty years ago.

'Morning John,' said the elder of the two mechanics.

'Believe it or not, but the van brought in a *nearside* lamp unit this morning and they haven't got the bearing shells for the 375.'

'Well you will just have to rob the car in the showroom for the lamp unit,' said John. 'We can't let Jones down again, and get Jane to ring round for the bearing shells. That car's been off the road for a fortnight now. And will you sweep this floor up. The factory rep is coming in at midday.'

The phone in his office was ringing, and John ran back to answer it. It was Mrs Jones who could not start her car to run her husband in to pick up his own. He had told her in the summer that it needed a new battery, but somehow they had never managed to get the car in to get it fitted. The service manager was busy checking in cars for service and John could not spare the mechanics so he would have to go himself.

A young woman in a dark raincoat who might just possibly have been a policewoman bore down on him in the corridor.

'Mr Heslop?'

'Yes,' he said.

'Good morning. Inland Revenue Recovery Station, Nashbourne. Computer Centre have notified us that your PAYE for October is still outstanding. It is supposed to be in by the 19th of the following month, you know. Can I take it with me?'

'Well it went off the day before yesterday. I know because I posted it myself. It must have arrived by now. We were a day or two late this month because my daughter, who does the books, is having to run the cash desk. Why didn't you telephone. Have you come all the way from Nashbourne?'

John felt a flush of annoyance. If this woman is at all officious, I'll bite her head off, he thought. Mrs Jones will be ringing again soon to know where I am.

'Yes, it's our new instructions Mr Heslop. We have to record a personal visit in each case. Some people get quite nasty about it, I can tell you. We've had to visit many firms we've never seen before, like yours. Of course some people delay as long as they can, but they are the ones who are never in when you call. Comes down from on high, they're tightening up you see.'

'All right, dear, will you see my daughter over there. She will give you a cheque number — that ought to satisfy them. I'm late for an appointment. It's really the Post Office's fault. They're the government themselves, after all,' he threw over his shoulder as he went out of the side door to the car.

By the time John got back and had seen Mr Jones off, it was 11 o'clock. There had been several telephone calls but he left them for the moment and started to open his mail. There were the usual circulars, the monthly statement from the oil company (the petrol had to be paid for by direct debit on delivery, you got no credit from them), service bulletins, and spares price increase notifications from the manufacturer, several bills, a bank statement that was worse than he had expected, some drawings and a quotation for some galvanized press work for the trailers that he was planning for, a VAT statement that did not look right and would need checking, a long form from the local authority about rate reassessment and an estimated corporation tax demand.

He looked at the tax demand wistfully. If only he was doing as well as they assumed, he could take the afternoon off. Of course there would not be any corporation tax liability at all when it came down to it. What little there was was taken out in drawings by himself, his wife and daughter. There was no point in declaring a profit and paying corporation tax (and then paying tax on dividends to yourself), not unless you wanted to pay no dividends and retain money in the business. He wished he could do that, but they were not making enough. His family's drawings were no bigger than his salary had been at Laidlows, years ago, although they did not spend much on food and nothing on motoring out of taxed income. Some of his friends on salaries were always grumbling about the tax they paid. John was not paying much at the higher rates in most years — even so it was money that could usefully have gone into the business in working capital. Fixed capital expenditure you could write off against profit, but not the new equity he had to keep putting in to meet the overhead that was going up all the time. The biggest tax of all, it sometimes seemed, was the tax on his time, looking after the government's requirements, and finding ways round them or through them and understanding their forms.

There were three letters, one with a French stamp which he opened first. This was what he had been waiting for. Yes, it was good news. An agricultural machinery dealer just across the channel that John had met through Jane's boyfriend was giving him an order for 20 trailers - £6,500 worth of business! There was a boom in trailers at the moment. DIY people were buying them to collect materials at trade prices, campers needed them for holidays and there was a steady demand from market gardeners, farmers and builders. The French were a bit behind in lightweight trailer design. John had designed a flat-bed half-ton trailer with a removable one-piece box in reinforced fibreglass. He used a fully welded frame with 13″ wheels and some of the running gear from the cars he was agent for. He had made a few one-offs at very high prices and these had gone and he could see how easily costs could be cut for longer runs. There was of course competition from the big people, but John's trailers were of very high quality; he had developed a 12 mm ply and steel skin floor panel that was easy to clean and practically indestructible.

The other two letters were bad news. It looked as if there was going to be trouble over the customer who had a front wheel blow-out on the M27 and who was holding Heslop Motors responsible. In fact they had repaired a front wheel inner tube some months ago but they would have to prove it was that one that failed. He was pretty sure the wheels had been moved round since, but it was a worry hanging over him. The other letter was infuriating. It was from the town architect specifying that an asbestos proof door had to be installed in the kitchen unit in the corridor at the rear of the showroom. What the fire risk was in a sink without even a hot tap, John could not think. A sliding door there would cost quite a bit. The answer, he supposed, was to remove the electric point for the kettle next to the sink and then it would not be a 'kitchen', but it would take months to get them to see it.

John had a beer and a sandwich with the factory service representative. When he got back, there were more calls but he had to go and see his accountant. He drove over — at this time of the year there would be no trouble parking. He loved the town in the autumn, the sea was a little choppy today and layer-coloured: deep blue out to the horizon, bottle green nearer in, with muddy yellow fingers where the sandbanks were. A few leaves of lighter yellow still hung on the trees in the wide street leading down from the front. Bob's office was in one of the big Georgian houses near the bottom of the street. 'B. Keen Chartered Accountant' was picked out in faded gold on the black-painted lower half of the window. There were very few people about, just a group of affluent French students. One of the girls was strikingly nice to look at in dark corduroy trousers beautifully cut, a black sweater as dark as her hair and with expensive looking shoes and a matching shoulder bag. There must be a lot of money to be made in language schools, John thought: there were two in the town, both booked solid, he had heard, until the end of next year. It helped the landladies fill up their boarding houses in the winter, too.

The front door of the house was open and John went straight in past the reeded glass reception window and upstairs into his friend's office. Bob's desk, unlike John's, was absolutely clear except for a neat pile of files at the corner. He did not have a Pirelli calendar hanging on the wall like John, nor a dirty ashtray, nor boxes of oil filters and valve caps gathering dust, but a good brown carpet, well dusted surfaces and an old glass-fronted bookcase full of books about business finance and tax law. Bob was a small, pale, slightly effeminate man with a kind smile. John owed much of his success to him. From the start Bob had insisted upon a quarterly accounting statement for the business. This showed the total net sales for the three months. Subtracted from this were paid out costs such as purchases of spares, petrol and so on, to give a figure for contribution to overheads (the rent, light, staff salaries and national insurance etc.) and gross profit (including his own and family's drawings and interest payments). A comparison of this contribution figure with an annual budget for overheads divided by four gave John a rough idea of how much he could afford to draw and how well or badly he was doing after allowance for his interest payments to the bank. He afterwards discovered that this was, in fact, a much more sophisticated accounting system than other business friends used.

At first, the quarterly statements had all seemed an unnecessary amount of work, because he could carry a running total of the monthly cash inflows and outflows in his head and knew how well he was doing. But as the business got larger – especially when the restaurant opened – he could feel the details slipping away from him. Taxation, he soon realized, was a major complication that he just could not work through in his head. Since his weekly sales fluctuated enormously – he might sell three

new cars one week and then none for a month or more —
his contributions to overheads and thus his gross profit
also moved up and down violently. So his annual profit,
which was what determined the tax he paid and thus how
much he could afford to draw, or reinvest in the business,
was completely uncertain at the beginning of the year.
After the first quarter his guess at the annual profit
outturn was not reliable to within plus or minus 200 per
cent. As the year went by this uncertainty diminished, but
even by the end of the year at best Bob could not tell him
within 25 per cent what his drawings after tax should have
been. There were several problems: the audit often
produced all sorts of write-offs and these never seemed to
be foreseeable; then there was uncertainty, especially when
the business was growing and changing, about how the
Inland Revenue would assess certain kinds of transactions.
The tax provisions themselves were changing all the time.
There was also uncertainty about how much working
capital the business needed; much of the addition to this
had to come out of taxed income. To make it all worse,
because the income tax rates were sharply progressive, a
small error in the net profit calculation could have a
disproportionate effect upon the amount of tax actually
payable.

The Revenue themselves had not finalized assessments
for his accounts for the previous three years, which was
another difficulty. (VAT was not clear cut either. An
inspector last week had come in to look at the VAT records
and had told him that credit card slips were not acceptable
as evidence of payment of input tax for petrol purchases
unless they bore the seller's VAT number — which of
course most of them did not. This had cost the firm a
hundred pounds or so of VAT paid but which could not be
reclaimed. It was not worth going back to the twenty or
more sellers involved to get duplicate receipts.)

Knowing Bob, and the Revenue, the tax provisions he

had made for past years were probably over-generous, but for the current year, which was only half-way through, the position was far from clear. Still, when you were worrying about every pound you spent, it seemed mad not to know even within thousands how much you actually had. He did not really understand it any more, consciously at least, and if he did not he was quite sure no one else did either. Bob had that sort of accountant's mind that happily assumes away uncertainty. John just did it by feel but felt like a circus performer on a high wire; if he looked down he would fall off. Funnily enough, the uncertainty was a challenge and the fact that ultimately he alone had to cope with it gave him a certain feeling of security.

John's problem today was just that. He wanted to know whether he could afford to go into the trailer business. He had an order and prospects of others, he had solved the technical problems and lined up suppliers, there was a large old farm building at the end of the site behind the restaurant where he could build them − if the local authority would give planning permission. Could he raise the capital for the equipment he needed, the repair and fitting out of the building and the material purchases? There were several other questions that Bob could not help with, such as whether he could get the welder and fitter he would need, but finance, as usual, was the first thing he had to settle.

'You are running somewhat ahead of last year,' said Bob. 'The restaurant is remarkably steady and fairly predictable now, though I agree the garage doesn't look so good at the moment. I reckon you should have £5,000 or so spare if you keep your drawings at current levels and there is a couple of thousand back tax due to you. I've just had the assessments through this morning. Have you worked out more carefully what you think you need?'

'I haven't got it written out, or calculated in detail but it's £20,000 minimum. The repairs to that big roof will be

£3,000 plus and for the building as a whole it will be at least £7,000. Then there's the tools and equipment, another £10,000: we shall have to have a hoist and gantry, the jigs we can make ourselves. Stocks of materials will be £2,000 and there's a tooling charge for that presswork for the floor pan. I'll have to buy in the box bodies. There's too much equipment needed to do those ourselves to start with.'

'Mmm, doesn't sound to me as if you have allowed anything for wages: two extra men for say six months, that's well over £3,500. Sounds more like £25,000 to me. I've looked at your figures. The margins look all right and you should make a reasonable profit, if you can get the orders, after allowing for servicing the additional capital. I think the bank would let you have another £15,000. I was talking to the manager last week. Of course you'd have to give directors' guarantees. But we'll still have to find another £4,000 or so.'

'Well, I could borrow on those with profits insurance policies I took out after the war,' said John. 'There's plenty enough there and it's cheaper than bank money.'

'You could do that. The other alternative is that we could try a venture capital house. Your total business is big enough for them to be interested though they might think you were over-diversifying at this stage.'

'Yes, but don't they want an equity stake and a director on the Board?'

'Probably, though not necessarily for such a small amount and you would keep control. They would provide loan capital too. The director would provide useful advice and contacts and he wouldn't interfere, you know, at least while things went well.'

'Oh, I don't like the idea of giving up equity and having some chap from London telling me what to do. I don't like directors' guarantees on a further bank loan, either. I'm in pretty deep Bob. I was thinking this morning if I broke a leg we'd be in real trouble. Limited liability's all right if you don't need to borrow and you go bust and leave a few suppliers holding the baby, but the way we are I'd lose everything: even the flat is owned by the company.'

'Well, you could go slower. You could just leave the trailer thing for a year or two. Or, you could probably sell off the garage as a going concern to Southsmith Motors if the oil company would play ball: you're always complaining about what a headache it is. You would make a nice capital gains and keep at least 70 per cent of it after tax. As I've already told you I'm not sure you can manage the garage and the trailer business and help the lads build the blessed trailers and do the buying for the restaurant and all the other things you are up to.'

'Yes, I've been thinking about that. The garage still wouldn't stand the cost of a really first class manager if I moved over more or less full time to the rest of the business, burdened as we are with those interest charges. There is plenty of scope for developing the trailer business and I've got some ideas for wholesale importing of food products and supplying other restaurants with fresh fish. I'm getting older too and still not putting much away for a pension. You keep telling me it comes off the top slice of tax, but I still have to find the money: there seem to be so many demands on the resources I've got. Thank you Bob, I'll think it over. I'll also see if we can't cut down on that tooling and equipment. To start with we could probably get away with something simpler. 'Bye.'

John walked out into the darkening street. He wanted to get home to talk to Margaret. Tea was about the only time they really had together. As he turned left onto the front he saw that the layered colours of the sea had changed and darkened too, but there was still a shimmer of red left on the horizon.

CHAPTER 3

Small Firms and their Problems

What is a Small Firm?

It troubles many people that there should be doubt
about exactly what a small firm is. It is quite clear what it is
not: ICI is not a small firm, nor is General Motors.
Provided we are at least clear that we are talking about
independent units of economic activity, there is also little
room for confusion at the other end of the scale: a
housewife who earns a little money as an agent for a mail-
order house, a small shopkeeper, a partnership of two
solicitors, a garage, a printing firm with six employees,
these are all small firms. The difficulty arises as we move
up the scale and it seems at first sight that small is, after all,
only a relative thing: a regional group of shops with six
branches is obviously small compared with Marks and
Spencers with approaching 300 branches, yet it is still a
large organization compared with the independent shop on
the corner.

On examination it is clear that at the bottom end of the
scale virtually all firms have at least one thing in common:
they are managed personally by the people that own them.
This is, in fact, the *essential* characteristic of the small
firm: the people that run it are those that bear the risks of
the enterprise. Owner-management is a necessary but not a
sufficient condition for a firm to be small, however, since

several very large firms can be wholly owned or controlled by the individuals which manage them or at least by their families. Examples are Ford, J. Sainsbury, C. & J. Clark and Getty Oil, none of which can be thought of as a small firm.

The importance of small firms in economic analysis – which it will take most of the rest of this book to demonstrate – also depends upon their absolute and relative size as well as upon the characteristic of owner-management. An economist's definition of a small firm, as the Bolton Report (1971)* stated, has also to allow for the factors which can limit the size of a firm. Thus a small firm is one that has only a small share of its market, is managed in a personalized way by its owners or part-owners and not through the medium of an elaborate management structure and which is not sufficiently large to have access to the capital market for the public issue or placing of securities. Once a firm has grown significantly beyond any, or all, of these three thresholds (market share, personal management and full access to all sources of capital) it will cease, for our purposes, to be a small firm.

It will be noted that our definition of a small firm has to exclude subsidiaries of larger companies. The management of a firm which is controlled by another, larger firm may well have a minority shareholding (though usually it will not) and it may have considerable freedom of action while it remains profitable, but it is essentially a branch of a larger enterprise with access to capital and perhaps technical assistance from the parent company and it will not be allowed to fail unless the parent company so decides. In British census statistics an important distinction is drawn between an *enterprise*, which is 'one or more firms under common ownership' and an

---

*The Committee of Inquiry on Small Firms under the chairmanship of John Bolton was appointed by Anthony Crosland in 1968.

establishment, which is a reporting unit, usually a physically independent factory or branch which is owned by an enterprise. Most small firms or enterprises own only one establishment, but the largest firms own literally hundreds of establishments.

Of the three thresholds, market share is the most ambiguous. It is another essential characteristic of a small firm that it cannot significantly influence its market because it faces too many competitors, it is, literally, at the mercy of market forces. Whilst a small firm may have a large share of a local market or a narrowly defined national market – it may have the only shop in a village for example, or be the only UK producer of eighteenth-century reproduction microscopes – there will be competition from other firms at some distance and potential competition from new firms if it attempts to operate on higher margins than similar firms elsewhere. By definition, the cost of setting up a new small firm is normally relatively low so that the threat of potential competition is a very real one. Although large firms also face actual and potential competition the impact of market forces is less brutal. A large firm can influence its markets by advertising or by controlling sales outlets and when the largest firm raises its prices its competitors will often conveniently follow. Large firms have the resources to diversify out of declining industries and are often too important as employers for governments to neglect when they get into trouble.

Personal management also follows from small size. Small firms cannot afford an elaborate management structure and do not need one. Whilst the owners, if there is more than one, will share responsibilities between them and may delegate some functions to managers, supervisors or professional advisors, they will none the less participate in all the principal decisions and will, typically, know what is going on in all parts of their business. The exact point at which a firm ceases to be managed by its owners in this sense is indeterminate, varying from industry to industry, firm to firm and with the individuals concerned and is not important. What is important is that in a small firm the people who take the risks are the owners and are therefore fully identified with the business in every sense. Although there are exceptions, as noted, ownership and management are separated in most large firms. Typically, the directors of a quoted company will own less than 5 per cent of the share capital, the bulk being in the hands of insurance companies, pension funds and thousands of small investors.

The owners are also normally the only source of additional equity capital in a small firm and loan capital is normally restricted to bank money secured by specific assets or an owner's personal guarantee. On this criteria the upper limit for a small firm might be quotation on the stock exchange, but here again a concrete definition is of little use. What really characterizes a small firm in this sense is that all its capital resources are strictly limited and this is not true of some large unquoted companies which are able to place securities privately, among institutional investors, raise loans abroad and obtain bank finance without the personal guarantees of the owners.

Ultimately, therefore, small firms are difficult to define because in the market economy the unit organization of economic activity is a continuum, running from the part-time housewife through to the multinational company with no clear break points. Legal form, whether it be sole trader, partnership, private or public company, is of little relevance since, except perhaps for the first example, that form offers no reliable guide to market share, management structure or access to capital.

In practice, economists and legislators alike are obliged to make arbitrary statistical definitions. The Bolton Committee defined a small firm in manufacturing as an enterprise with 200 employees or less and in retailing one with an annual turnover of £50,000 or less (at 1963 prices). In Continental Europe, it is usual to distinguish between small and medium enterprises (Petites et Moyennes Entreprises (PME)); in manufacturing small enterprises are those with 50 employees or less and medium with 51-300 employees. In the United States, the Small Business Act (1953) states that 'a small business concern shall be deemed to be one which is independently owned and operated and which is not dominant in its field of operation'. The Small Business Administration (SBA) uses its powers under this Act to define small business in terms of employees and turnover at various levels according to industry. Thus American Motors, a substantial enterprise with 28,000 employees, has been classified as a small firm because it has only 2 per cent of the US car market.

What Small Firms Do

Despite the decline in their number and share in economic activity over the last half century, small firms remain numerous and important. The Bolton Committee estimated that according to its own definition of the term and including agriculture, forestry, fishing and the professions, in 1963 there were about 1¼ million small firms in the UK employing about 6 million people. This was equivalent to 25 per cent of the employed population and small firms accounted for nearly 20 per cent of the GNP. There is no reason to suppose that these figures are very different today.

Table 3.1 gives a more recent estimated breakdown of total employment in small firms by sector showing the percentage of private sector employment accounted for by small firms. The popular impression that small firms are mainly engaged in providing services rather than in making things is not borne out by the facts, although a small

TABLE 3.1: UK employment in small firms by sector, mid-1976

	Numbers employed in small firms ('000)	Employed in small firms as per cent of total employment in the private sector	Per cent of total employment in small firms
Manufacturing	1,549	22	27.9
Distributive trades	1,236	39	22.2
Miscellaneous services	1,101	43	19.8
Construction	732	49	13.2
Professional and scientific services	373	48	6.7
Insurance, banking, finance and business services	231	20	4.2
Agriculture, forestry and fisheries	195	30	3.5
Transport and communications	112	21	2.0
Mining, quarrying, gas, electricity and water	28	49	0.5
ALL SMALL FIRMS	5,557	32	100.0

NOTE: Includes the self-employed and employers. Estimated from official censuses using Bolton definitions or those of *Enterprise into the Eighties*, CBI, 1977.

majority of all small firms are in service industries. Manufacturing easily provides the largest employment in small firms although their share of total employment in that sector is only 22 per cent. Within manufacturing, small firms are represented everywhere, for example, the largest sub-sector for employment in small firms is mechanical engineering which is the largest sector in manufacturing, but they tend to be less important in industries which require large amounts of capital such as chemicals and heavy electrical engineering. The capital required for a new job in a small manufacturing firm is now probably well over £5,000; in a very large firm it may be between five and ten times as much, though on average the firm with more than 200 employees spends about 50 per cent more in capital expenditure per employee than one employing less than 200.

The variety of activities upon which small firms are engaged in manufacturing, the circumstances in which they operate and the role they play in the manufacturing economy are unfamiliar to most people and impossible to appreciate from a study of statistics. The author, in the course of a study of small firms for the European Commission interviewed a sample of small firms in the British engineering industries in the summer of 1979 and some examples from this source will help put some flesh on the bones of the statistics. One firm employing 40 people was manufacturing dies and presses for sintering (a process in which metal powder is compressed between dies to form strong and accurate metal components). It had an international reputation in this particular form of precision manufacture and it was developing and supplying tools to large engineering concerns all over the world. Another firm of about the same size had developed advanced methods for flame profiling of heavy plate (cutting out thick sheets of steel). Both these firms were innovating and helping large firms to substitute new and cheaper forms of fabrication for components which a few years ago would have been made from castings or forgings.

Another firm, employing only four people, in a converted pig sty, had designed and manufactured a new type of air valve for safety helmets and had found a method for machining a particular type of cylinder liner for internal combustion engines that had defeated the development department of at least one large motor manufacturer. Another tiny rural firm was machining precision components for the Bloodhound missile and wheels for model railway engines in a workshop rented from a road haulage company. Other small firms interviewed were manufacturing and marketing electronics products, some of them for small and specialized markets, some in direct competition with large firms.

The activities of small firms in construction, in farming, quarrying or transport are more familiar, though here, too, there may be some surprises. The small transport company down the road may be delivering purpose-built machinery overland to the Middle East. The small farmer, if you have not visited one lately, may well have £100,000 worth or more of surprisingly large and complicated equipment in his barn and only two or three employees to work 500 acres. In financial and business services, a very rapidly expanding field for small firms, there are insurance brokers, computer software houses and specialists in a wide range of activities from, for example, direct mail services and public relations consultants, to the servicing of office equipment and head hunters.

Small firms in the distributive trades (wholesaling and retailing), miscellaneous services (which includes pubs and cafes, shoe repairers, garages, cinemas and dry cleaners) and professional and scientific services (doctors, lawyers, vets and secretarial colleges, for example) are, of course, more familiar still and need no elaboration.

Statistics on small firms in most of these activities are

very inadequate. Some data are collected on a sample basis selected from registers which cannot be comprehensive, especially for tiny enterprises and are impossible to keep up to date. There are also censuses which aim at completeness but which also depend upon the same registers and are in any event taken only at long intervals with the results appearing several years later. There are other problems. One is that there is no enterprise census in the UK, only a series of sector censuses, but some small establishments in some sectors are actually owned by firms in other sectors so that we get double counting if we add together the small firms in each of the separate inquiries, as we were obliged to do in Table 3.1 for want of any better alternative.

At first sight it might appear that government statisticians have several sources against which they could check their registers of small firms: returns of income to the Inland Revenue, the VAT register, and all sorts of administrative procedures that involve contacts between government and small firms. In fact, however, the power of government departments to use information supplied in confidence for one purpose or another or to pass it on to another department is heavily circumscribed by law even where, as is frequently the case, that information is not subject to serious limitations for statistical purposes.

Another problem with small firm statistics is that many small firms, though mainly sole proprietorships, that is self-employed persons, are not included at all while part of the sales and income of more substantial small firms is omitted. This is the so-called Black Economy, black because VAT is not paid on sales nor is income declared to the Inland Revenue; its transactions are wholly or partly in cash or kind.

By definition the Black Economy is not included in official statistics, although partly because some black income is spent in 'white' shops there is a discrepancy in the national accounts between the size of the GDP measured in terms of expenditure and that measured by output or income. A personal estimate by a Commissioner of the Inland Revenue is that 7.5 per cent of the GDP is generated in the Black Economy, but of course there is no way in which this estimate can be verified. Underground economic activity seems to be growing if such indicators as the issue of large denomination bank notes are any guide.

Risk and Reward

The existence of the Black Economy is a useful corrective to those who romanticize excessively about small firms and their proprietors. There is, of course, a romantic side to the struggles of the lone entrepreneur. There are still plenty of examples of fortunes being made from beginnings in small firms, and the successful business founder and manager is, as we are trying to argue in this book, playing an absolutely essential role in the market economy. If society was aware how essential this entrepreneur is to economic growth (and if it really cared about economic growth) then it would make him the hero-figure of our time. For starting up a business of one's own requires courage and tenacity as well as skill, and it involves great risk. The odds are well stacked against success, since in the United States about 50 per cent of new ventures fail in the first two years and only a tiny minority last ten years. Even then research suggests that changes in economic prosperity or market conditions can bring a small firm down at any time: survival for ten years does not, it seems, produce a lower probability of failure in year 11 than in year 10.

Business failure is not a trivial matter. It should not be over-looked that the proprietor of a small firm which fails, loses his livelihood and is not, as a formerly self-employed person, eligible for the dole. Whether they involve bankruptcy or not, most business failures result in heavy personal loss for the entrepreneur. It is virtually impossible to start a business entirely on other people's money and it is very common for entrepreneurs to remortgage or even sell their houses to raise the necessary capital. Even where this is not done, personal guarantees are often necessary for bank borrowings or property leases and if the business fails, realization of personal assets may be necessary to meet these guarantees. To this extent the protection offered by limited liability is circumvented. Apart from the anguish of having to dismiss loyal employees and the realization that much hard work and dedication has come to nothing, the failed businessman receives little sympathy and, if the liquidation of his firm is involuntary, whether he as an individual is declared bankrupt or not, there is undeniable social disapproval. Indeed bankruptcy in Britain, though not in the United States, does nearly as little for social standing as a prison sentence.

Alas, in Britain, there is here an asymmetry which does not exist in other more prosperous countries, in that success, although invariably gratifying, often does not meet with universal approbation. One research study has shown that in contemporary British society working people who successfully start their own firm may find themselves ostracized by their former colleagues and that a desire to minimize this sometimes acts as a brake upon further expansion. Success and the problems of success often also lead to the break-up of business partnerships and of marriages which are, in any event, often threatened by the long hours and preoccupation that running a small business involves.

There are other risks in small business. The ordinary, law-abiding citizen whose previous brushes with the law are confined to parking offences will find, in starting his own firm, that he is confronted with a battery of unfamiliar and complex legal requirements of which complete mastery is impossible and to which his conscience is a most inadequate guide. The Tax Acts, the Factory Acts, the Fair Trading Acts, company legislation, weights and measures, are just a few of the things that have to be complied with. Since the law cannot be fully understood by the layman there is always the risk that he is breaking it unwittingly. It is doubtful if it is possible to run a small business today without breaking the law in at least a technical sense though in practice officials are very sympathetic to unintended breaches of the law.

Finally, there is the question of provision for old age. Most new businesses are probably, and advisedly, started by persons of mature years. The capital requirements of a growing business are such that although the tax treatment of pension contributions is extremely generous, the entrepreneur will typically find it difficult to make adequate provision for himself, especially in his early years when these contributions can produce most ultimate benefit. If he is self-employed in a legal sense (that is his business is unincorporated) he will not even be eligible to contribute to the state graduated pension. If his business fails when he is still below pensionable age but is too old to get employment easily, he may face a difficult time, even if he has been able to make a reasonable level of contributions to a private pension scheme. If he has not been able to do this then he faces old age on the basic State pension.

Given all these risks and the difficulties of success: acquiring the necessary knowledge in his chosen field, identifying a market opportunity, assembling the necessary resources, producing and marketing his product or service, it is perhaps remarkable that anyone goes into small business at all.

Quite a lot is now known about the characteristics of business founders. Their motivations and typology are clearly complex. The unifying characteristic is that they are individualists with strong drives towards self-expression and independence. However, these inner drives are frequently not enough; external events, more often than not, force the entrepreneur to take the major step of setting up on his own. Most of them gain experience initially by working for others, in the vast majority of cases in another small business where they learn the problems and opportunities at first hand. Some of them nurse a long-term ambition to work for themselves and save and plan for it, but these are probably the minority. Most are probably vaguely dissatisfied with their jobs but are not sure why and not sure what the alternatives are, and are pitched into self-employment by some catalytic event. The firm they are working for may collapse: the high death rate in small firms, in which most of them worked before starting up on their own, makes this a common event. Other stimuli may be less brutal, for example, a disagreement with their boss over the wisdom of embarking on a new product, a merger of their firm with another or an inheritance.

Several studies in a variety of countries show that the small business founder is typically socially disadvantaged in some way (Bannock and Doran 1978). A high proportion of immigrants, as is well known, run a large proportion of small retailing establishments in urban areas. Indigenous entrepreneurs come from broken homes or have interrupted education even where they do have a favoured social background. A large group of business founders, particularly in manufacturing, consists of people with a skilled working-class background who have set up on their own doing what they previously did for an employer sometimes on a subcontracted basis. The business founder is not typically an articulate, polished member of whatever part of society happens to be the elite of the day: these tend to go into the professions, the civil service or large firms where their social and educational skills assure them a good chance of success with little risk. It is very often the desperate, the nonconformist and the odd man out that goes into small business. Of course, some members of the elite will also go into small business but closer examination will invariably show that they were uncomfortable in their preordained place at the top of the establishment.

The small businessman, then, seems to be typically something of a misfit in social terms and needs to prove himself by establishing his own sphere of activity where he is free of the will of others. (Actually he soon finds that his boss is the customer, but at least he is dealing with the boss directly.) All the evidence points to the high value placed on independence by small firm proprietors: money, though important, is a secondary motivation. Many people working for themselves could make more in the employment of others. Few people having successfully built their own business want to work for someone else even though they might make more by doing so.

Frequently, a man who has been successful and then sells out to a large firm, continuing as an employee, will chafe at the prison he has made for himself and leave the security of salaried employment to start up on his own again. Most in this position probably cannot perform at their best when following the will of others. They suspect or know that they will perform best when they follow their own instincts. It is not so much that a small firm proprietor cannot explain and persuade (he will be persuasive enough with his customers though he may lack the skill to do so on paper — something which is important in a large bureaucratic organization) but he seems to work largely on intuition and it is difficult to justify intuition to others. For the same reasons he will find it difficult to delegate to others: a possibility which, in any event is denied to the proprietor of a very small firm.

Finance

It is vitally important to bear in mind this picture of the mentality and situation of the small businessman in discussing his problems and the possible solutions to them. The key problem, given the will to start a business, is usually finance. The entrepreneur has to find enough money to support himself and his family until he begins to generate adequate income from the business. He has to find the capital to pay rent or buy premises, to fit them out and to purchase stock and equipment. If he is going to have employees from the outset then he needs more working capital to pay their wages. He has to allow for the fact that unless he is in the retail trade his customers will not expect to pay their bills immediately, though most of his suppliers will give him some credit.

All this takes a lot of money, several thousand pounds at least, and it is difficult to accumulate that out of taxed income as an employee. Virtually the only institutional source of funds at this stage will be his bank. His bank manager may agree to a small unsecured overdraft and will probably lend him more if he has security, such as a house or some stocks and shares. One other possibility may be a loan from an insurance company against an endowment policy. It sounds very risky and indeed for most people practically impossible, unless they can find a rich relation or partner who will back them or unless they inherit money.

In practice, other solutions are often found to the problem of raising capital. In many cases businesses are started on a part-time basis, so that risk is minimized and some income still comes in. One of a married couple will continue to work, some assets can be sold (one small business recently was started on the proceeds of the sale of a cherished vintage car). A second mortgage on the house may release a surprisingly large amount of capital (an increasingly common solution this, in these days of inflation). Some people will have redundancy money or will be able to retire early with a pension and perhaps a lump sum. (These too are increasingly common sources of start-up finance.) A pub or club will start with a loan from a brewer, from credit or even a contract with stage payments from a previous employer. There are really quite a surprising range of possibilities.

Someone who wants to start a small business in a field where fairly substantial amounts of capital are required may first need to gain experience and accumulate funds in another kind of business. No more instructive example of this route can be found than that of Mr Lucius Carey, the editor and proprietor of the *Venture Capital Report*, a subscription publication which gives details of small businesses which are seeking capital. Mr Carey left business school with the intention of starting an engineering firm. He realized that he could not initially raise the substantial capital required for the engineering business and started a hamburger restaurant with the object of accumulating capital. He was successful and now has a small chain of these restaurants, but became so interested in the problem of raising capital for small firms that he started his *Venture Capital Report*. Incidentally the vast majority of the businesses which succeed in obtaining funds through mention in the Report do so from private individuals or other small businesses and not from financial institutions: no quoted company has yet backed anything, though several subscribe to the Report.

It will also be possible for the new businessman to minimize the amount of capital required. The familiar story of the entrepreneur who starts a manufacturing or electronics research business in his garden shed or garage is not a rare instance at all, it is very common: perhaps 30 per cent or more of such businesses start in that way. In only a few instances will a small business start with employees;

these come later. New machinery or equipment may be unnecessary, and the essential stuff may be picked up quite cheaply second-hand, perhaps from another small firm that has gone into liquidation.

Difficult as they are, the financial problems of starting a small business can be overcome and literally thousands are started in Britain every year. But survival and growth present other financial problems. A temporary downturn in demand, a fire, illness or some other misfortune can easily kill off a small business that is growing and basically sound. Its proprietor may have sunk all his capital into the firm and will have little left to tide him over a bad patch. Subject to their rules about security and risk, the bank may be sympathetic and helpful, but the bank manager, himself a member of a bureaucratic organization and without direct experience of running a business, may find it difficult to be too helpful for fear of getting sucked in to more lending than can be repaid. He may conclude that the business is 'undercapitalized' and press for liquidation. Even for an initially prosperous business, the tax system will prevent the proprietors from accumulating funds out of trading surpluses to see it through this sort of situation. A self-employed person or partnership – and most businesses start off with these legal forms – may find itself paying tax at 60 per cent (until recently it could have been much more) one year and the next no tax at all because it has a very small income. Corporation tax for companies, especially small companies, is lower but still reduces what can be accumulated in the business. Tax reliefs for investment do not help if a firm cannot afford to invest.

A new but healthy small firm with say five or ten employees will also find it difficult to raise capital for further expansion. What it really needs, given the risks it faces, is equity but there are virtually no sources of institutional finance of this type and even if there were the entrepreneur might be reluctant to use them for fear of losing his independence and freedom of action. He would be more amenable to giving equity to private individuals, particularly relations, but high rates of income and capital taxation may have reduced the numbers of Aunt Agathas who can invest in this way. High rates of taxation on dividends have certainly also diminished incentives for 'sleeping partners' to invest in small firms – they can get a better after-tax return with no risk by investing in government securities or by investing in quoted companies and property through insurance companies.

A growing small firm will be unlikely to be making sufficient profits to finance its own expansion. One reason for this has already been mentioned – taxes will slow down the rate at which funds can be accumulated. It is also probably true in times of high inflation that no way can be found of investing internally generated funds that, after tax, will keep up with the cost of new capital equipment. The problem is that investment in the growth of a small firm, particularly in manufacturing (financing problems in the service trades may be easier) is not typically required in regular small amounts but in a series of discrete jumps. A move to larger premises or the acquisition of a second machine tool will require a very large investment in relation to the capital base of a small firm.

Loan finance is, in most cases, the only practical solution to the finance of expansion for the type of small firms we are considering and this means recourse to the clearing banks. (Though in the countryside, the Council for Industries in Rural Areas (COSIRA) and elsewhere some other state organizations might help.) But banks will be reluctant to make loans to firms or individuals without a good track record (and a new firm cannot have one) especially where these loans are not matched by increases in equity. (UK banks like to see at least a 1:1 ratio for equity to loan capital in the balance sheet.) Even where they are willing to lend, they will require security which will typically be difficult for the small firm to provide. In their early stages of growth they probably do not own their premises and banks are often reluctant to take plant or stocks and work in progress as security.

In an article in *Lloyds Bank Review* (October 1979) Martin Binks pointed out the further difficulty that 'The size and age of the firm are often inversely related to the financial expertise of management. The proprietor may not have the skills necessary for producing the sophisticated cash-flow projections often required by the lender in order to assess the viability and potential of the borrower.' He summarized the problem of finance for the new small manufacturing firm in the form of a statement (Binks Law) which is, in fact, probably true for a much wider group of small firms than he intended: 'The smaller the firm, the larger the proportionate increase in capital base required to respond to an increase in demand, but the lower its ability to command loan and equity finance.'

As firms grow larger the incremental increase in capital required for each expansion tends to become proportionately less and the range of financial institutions and sources of equity open to it increases. Even without rapid growth a lengthening record of expansion and profit will strengthen the firm's case. At quite an early stage the Industrial and Commercial Finance Corporation (ICFC) is prepared to make loans or take equity and there are several other venture capital organizations, including the Small Business Capital Fund and, higher up the scale, Charterhouse Development Ltd. All these bodies normally have more funds than they can profitably invest and the UK probably has a better range of commercial facilities of this type than any other country. The problem at this level is that having achieved the demonstrable success in which financial institutions are then prepared to share, the small-medium firm owner-manager is even more reluctant to release equity or brook interference from outside than he was at the beginning. There may also be an information problem in that some small firms are not well informed about the sources of institutional finance. Certainly every time someone organizes a competition for new business ideas, all sorts of people crawl out of the woodwork with viable propositions in which institutions are prepared to invest. It also seems that new institutions and new services from existing institutions, of which there have been many since Bolton reported in 1971, attract takers, and it is a fact that the counsellors of the government Small Firm Service are turning up increasing numbers of small firm investment opportunities which are being taken up by financial institutions.

Much more could be said about the financial problems of small firms, but it would add little. These problems have been well aired in the reports of the successive official inquiries into the subject from Macmillan in 1932 to Wilson in 1979. Much of the research resources of recent inquiries have been devoted to a search for evidence that viable small firms are actually held back by lack of finance. This evidence − in the form of specific instances − is, of course, difficult to find since rapidly expanding small firms are by definition obviously solving their financing problems. The credit worthiness of those that are not is always open to doubt, while those that have not been started through lack of funds are impossible to identify, let alone assess. For similar reasons analysis of the accounts of samples of small firms is not very illuminating. Whilst research of this kind does suggest that small firms, particularly fast growing firms, rely on borrowing only a little more than large firms, the existence of conventions about the levels of gearing (borrowing in relation to capital employed) which are acceptable, as well as limitations in the availability of loan capital, clearly affect ratio comparisons of this sort. All we can say is that most of the evidence suggests that most small firms that do succeed are regarded as poor if not unacceptable credit risks at some stage in their growth, because this is inherent in the highly risky business of establishing a small firm. Since banks, the only effective source for very small firms, do not take risks (they admit to insignificant losses on lending to small firms) there is at the least a strong presumption that the establishment and expansion of small firms is held up by lack of bank finance, given that the growth of taxation and other changes have diminished the supply of funds from other sources.

Red Tape and Regulation

The problem most heard about from small firms is red tape and form-filling. There are forms to be filled in for the rating authorities, for changes in directorships, the filing of accounts or the issue of shares, there are VAT forms, Income Tax forms and statistical inquiry forms and many other administrative forms arising from measures to help small firms such as grants and other assistance. On top of this is all the legislation that has to be complied with. This has grown enormously in recent years. John Bolton, at an Institute of Bankers Conference in 1978, listed the legislation *in the employment field alone* which was enacted in the three years 1972-5 following the report of his Committee of Inquiry (which recommended action to cut down on government generated paperwork for small firms):

Contracts of Employment Act 1972 (subsequently amended by the Employment Protection Act 1975);
European Communities Act 1972 (enabling enforcement of the European Directives);
Social Security Act 1973;
Employment and Training Act 1973;
Health and Safety at Work Act 1974;

Trades Unions and Labour Relations Act 1974
(amended by a further Act in 1976);
Rehabilitation of Offenders Act 1974;
Social Security and Pensions Act 1975;
Industry Act 1975;
Employment Protection Act 1975;
Sex Discrimination Act 1975.

Quite apart from the difficulties created by the actual provisions of this legislation (which are referred to on p.47) the sheer volume and the work associated with it are seen as a major burden by small firm proprietors who, it must be appreciated, unlike their counterparts in large firms, normally have to cope alone. Matters are made worse because no attempt is made by the authorities to sort out what is relevant to small firms and what is not, nor is any real attempt made to express the legislation or, worse still, the explanatory leaflets, in clear and simple language. Most of the readers of this book will probably never have actually read an Act of Parliament. Those affecting small businesses are commonly 200 or more pages in length expressed in the following kind of language (one sentence from the Development Land Tax Act 1976):

Where, by virtue of any provision of the Income Tax Acts, income tax under Schedule D in respect of the profits or gains of a trade for any year of assessment is to be computed by reference to the amount of the profits or gains of some other period and, as a result, more than one year of assessment is, by virtue of the preceding provisions of this paragraph, an affected year by reason of the same deduction under sub-paragraph (1) above, the payments which are treated as having been received as mentioned in sub-paragraph (7) above in respect of each of those affected years shall be treated as all being received in the last of those affected years; but in any other case a payment so treated as having been received in respect of an affected year shall be treated as having been received in that year.

Of course, VAT forms can be left to the book-keeper (if there is one) and the firm's accountant and solicitor can deal with much of the rest (at a price). Much of it has to be ignored however, because there just is not time to do anything else, but bureaucracy is an irritant, adding to responsibility and frustration and representing an intrusion, an interference which the entrepreneurial mentality finds it difficult to accept.

If you ask a sample of small firm proprietors what their problems are, taxation and red tape will usually be included in the answer, but so too will be sheer physical restraints to the growth of business: lack of premises or labour or finance. They also see government action (or inaction) as lying behind many of these restraints: planning regulations or urban redevelopment in the past have reduced the supply of cheap premises, incomes policies have reduced wage differentials and contributed to labour shortages, excessive social security has reduced the incentive to work, taxation has prevented the accumulation of capital and high interest rates inhibit borrowing.

The various acts governing conditions of employment are a particular bugbear of small firms. Proprietors, with justification, feel that the law on Unfair Dismissal places the employer in the position of being guilty unless he can prove otherwise. Some feel that redundancy provisions have effectively made labour a fixed cost rather than a variable cost. It seems unlikely that labour legislation has had a major effect upon the willingness of small firms to take on labour, but it must have had some effect.

Small firm proprietors are for the most part, of course, anti-collectivist, anti-trade union, anti-government and can hardly be expected to enjoy being taxed, so it is not surprising that they blame much of their problems on the government (or on the unions). We have seen, however, that there are also deeper reasons for associating the decline of small business with the growth of government. In particular the growth of taxation has distorted capital markets while mistaken policies of support for large firms have also played a part. Is it all the fault of the growth of governments, then? However complex, is that all there is to it?

Social Values

It would probably be wrong to lay the whole of the blame for the decline of small business at the door of the government. It is true that government has grown everywhere and with it small business has declined everywhere, (as shown in Chapter 4) and there do seem to be differences that could be explained by differences in specific government policies towards small business. Nevertheless the decline of small business, like the growth of democratic government itself, can be traced partly to the subtle effects of affluence, a deeper cause that has its roots in developing knowledge and technology. For affluence has brought with it greater material security and an even greater valuation of security. Social values have moved away from risk taking and have focused upon the costs of economic growth in which entrepreneurship plays such a crucial role and this has reduced the status of the small businessman. Education far more than taxation has levelled society and may have reduced the number of socially marginal people who need to prove themselves by building their own business. The education system, which reflects and reinforces social values, has prepared children for employment in large firms in the government and other large institutions and has done nothing to encourage the idea that they might work for themselves.

It is no coincidence that the harsher economic climate since the mid-1970s seems to have been associated with some recovery in the position of small business as well as a massive increase in public interest in it. In particular there seems to have been some increase in the rate of formation of new small firms not only in Britain but in Germany, Canada and other countries. Research by Johnson and Darnell of Durham University suggests that higher unemployment has historically been associated with more new business formation. Several historians (notably in France, Japan and Norway) claim that periods of economic depression seem, paradoxically, to have favoured small business. This may have something to do with the fact that people who cannot find work as employees will start up on their own but it also has to do with the greater availability of labour and other resources to existing small businesses. It may also be that greater pressure on cost competitiveness and the other new opportunities which recession offers in the obsolescence of much large scale activity favour the small firm. In any event, at a deeper level society has perceived the need for a change in emphasis in the organization and conduct of economic activity. The social instinct for survival is a sure and strong one.

CHAPTER 4

The International Dimension

Statistical Comparisons

Perhaps the thing which struck readers the most in the research findings of the Bolton Report was not that small firms were declining in Britain and other countries (the conventional wisdom was that this was inevitable with modern technology), but that the decline had gone further and faster in Britain than elsewhere.

If small firms in industry were outmoded and a sign of technological and economic immaturity, why were they more numerous and important in all other advanced countries, including the United States and Germany which were more advanced than the UK? If competing abroad and faster growth required the concentration of industry into bigger units, how was it that Japan and Italy could sustain exceptionally rapid growth in exports and output with a much bigger proportion of output in small firms than most other countries? How could a tiny country like Switzerland meet foreign competition and sustain high standards of living with twice the proportion of employment in small firms as the UK?

It was not that UK firms were heavily concentrated in

the middle range, had fewer small firms and fewer large firms. Of the world's 500 largest companies in the middle 1960s UK firms came second only to the United States. Britain had nearly as many multinationals in that list as the six countries of the EEC put together and considerably more than Japan. Britain's industry was, and probably still is, the most concentrated in the world.

Table 4.1 presents some more up-to-date data on the importance of small establishments in manufacturing in OECD countries. The relative importance of small firms has not changed very much between countries since the figures published by Bolton (which related mainly to the early 1960s). These figures show that the decline in the share of small establishments in employment has continued in about half the countries listed, though it has actually increased in Japan and Switzerland. However, since large firms have been acquiring small ones in all countries, on an enterprise basis the share of small firms in manufacturing employment probably declined virtually everywhere. There has been considerable growth in employment in small firms in service industries also. Since the middle 1970s, however, the world recession seems to have been accompanied by a slowing down and even a reversal in the decline of small firms.

At first glance the table does not suggest any clear relationship between economic performance and the importance of small firms. Contrary to earlier received wisdom, however, it is obvious that a high small firm ratio is consistent with either high levels of growth or output and that the UK is at the bottom of the table in all respects. Correlations of this kind are difficult to interpret even where the data are strictly comparable (which in this case they are not). Historical factors, natural resource endowment and all sorts of things other than industrial structure must influence economic growth. There are many technical factors which affect the comparability of data.

TABLE 4.1: The proportion of manufacturing employment in small establishments, GDP per head and rate of growth in GDP, selected OECD countries

	Proportion of manufacturing employment in small firms per cent		Real GDP per head US$ of 1970 PP	Annual compound rate of growth in real GDP per head 1950-78 per cent
Japan	65 (1966)	66 (1975)	3,578	7.3
Italy	66 (1961)	59 (1971)	2,880	4.1
Switzerland	61 (1965)	64 (1975)	4,292	2.5
Australia	60 (1963)		4,209	2.3
Norway	64 (1967)	58 (1975)	4,327	3.5
France	51 (1963)		4,383	3.8
Belgium	51 (1962)	45 (1975)	4,391	3.4
Netherlands	47 (1960)	42 (1977)	4,052	3.3
Canada	47 (1963)	44 (1975)	4,806	2.8
Sweden	53 (1965)	41 (1975)	4,695	2.6
US	39 (1963)	38 (1972)	5,160	2.2
Federal Republic of Germany	34 (1963)	31 (1976)	4,160	4.5
UK	31 (1963)	29 (1975)	3,572	2.1

SOURCE: National Statistical Offices. Dutch data relate to enterprises. German data exclude Handwerk. GDP data from Angus Maddison, *Per Capita Output in the Long Run*, Kylos, 1979 Fasc. 1/2 Small establishments are those employing 200 persons or fewer.

The German definition of establishment is less restrictive than the UK definition, for example, while German statistics which include 'Handwerk' include 'sausage' makers and other service-related activities, some of which (if they existed) would not be included in manufacturing in the UK. There also seem to be differences in the 'quality' of small firms in different countries though quality in this context is an elusive and possibly misleading concept. Willibrord Sauer of the German Handwerk Association has pointed out that many of the small manufacturing firms in France and Italy are not stable 'modern' enterprises but family based craft firms whose members earn less than the national minimum wage and which disappear in recession and re-emerge again in boom times. Other commentators suggest that much of Italy's recent export successes are attributable to small businesses operating in an underground economy. Certainly in Japan a large proportion, perhaps 40 per cent of small manufacturing firms, are subcontractors to large firms and have little independence.

In fact when larger numbers of countries (including developing countries) are examined, it seems that there is a clear tendency for both the rate of economic growth and the importance of small firms to decline as levels of income reach those of the richer advanced countries. It is clear that the achievement of high levels of wealth does not depend upon the reduction in the importance of small firms. It is rather that other factors associated with high living standards, notably the increased role of government, act as a brake upon the formation and growth of small firms. At the same time there are other factors which also combine to promote slower growth at high levels of affluence, for instance the emergence of social limits to growth and the more limited scope for productivity gains in the service industries (into which employment shifts from agriculture and manufacturing) (Bannock 1976).

The UK has a much smaller proportion of employment in small firms in manufacturing (and probably in non-manufacturing too) than would be expected from its level of economic development, while other countries, for example Japan and the United States, have larger small firm populations than might be expected.

It is a question of some importance as to whether Britain has fewer small firms than other countries because it has a lower birth rate for new enterprise or a higher death rate. The difficulty in answering this question is simply that very little information on entries to and exits from the small firm population is available for any country. The Bolton Committee calculated that new incorporations per thousand of the human population were lower in the UK than in the United States and that the death rate was higher though there was some evidence in these and later data that the death rate was declining and the birth rate increasing. The Committee also concluded from the available evidence that the average age of small firms was higher in the UK than in the US, although this could be consistent with either a lower birth rate or a lower death rate. Other data suggest that both birth and death rates of small enterprise are lower in the UK than elsewhere. Birth rates also appear to be higher than average in the more prosperous parts of Britain and other countries and lower in areas where the bulk of employment is concentrated in branch plants of large firms.

One particularly interesting finding of international research on the demography of small firms has been that the initial size of new enterprises seems to be declining in the long term, even though the average size of surviving small (and large) enterprises has been increasing. These findings are important and are consistent with the view that shortages of start-up capital are inhibiting the establishment of new firms.

Public Support for Small Firms

There have been no comprehensive studies of the legal and economic environments of small firms in various countries though the author has been commissioned to carry out such a study by Shell UK Ltd. (Bannock 1980) It is obvious, however, that the governments of most European countries as well as those of Japan and the United States have committed more effort and resources into promoting small business than Britain.

The German Federal government, for example, will spend £165 million on programmes to promote small firms in 1980, while the Länder (regional) governments will probably spend almost half as much. UK expenditures are a tiny fraction of these amounts, as is illustrated by the fact that the number of staff employed in the small firm sponsoring departments in the two countries are 25 in the UK and 200 in Germany. The Federal government's grant to the Small Firm Research Institute which carries out economic research into the subject is £280,000 per annum. Not included in these figures are interest rate subsidies from ERP funds for small firms or the value of various tax concessions given to small business.

While government attitudes, which reflect more clearly articulated philosophies on the economic and social importance of small business, are more favourable in other countries, the greater size of the small firm sector abroad is also favoured by greater independent initiatives to help small firms. Thus in many European countries, powerful chambers of commerce (membership of which is a legal obligation in several countries) play an important role in providing information and assistance for small firms. In Germany, Switzerland, Japan and other countries there are mutual assistance organizations which provide credit guarantees for small firms which wish to borrow from the banking system, but are unable to do so through lack of suitable collateral. Small firm representative bodies are also very much stronger in most other countries than they are in Britain.

The small firm problem and measures to promote small business are not confined to the developed countries. In the period immediately following World War II the developing world was also caught up in the fever for bigness in industrial organization. Development aid from the international agencies such as the World Bank was heavily concentrated in favour of large-scale infrastructural projects and resource exploitation involving joint ventures with multinational groups. If the advanced countries had oil refineries, large steel mills and chemical plants, so too must the poorer countries: it was assumed that the general path of development must be the same, but that the new developing countries could skip the stage of small-scale industry and pass directly to the concentrated industry of modern times. Disillusionment with this philosophy was soon to set in, not only because it meant heavy reliance upon foreign enterprise and capital, but because the development of capital intensive industry did nothing to help reduce unemployment nor did it ease the horrific problems of congestion and poverty in the big cities; in short it was not effective.

Although many developing countries, notably India and China, have long given attention to small-scale decentralized economic activity, emphasis is shifting increasingly towards small enterprise. Governments in the developing world and international agencies are now concentrating more upon getting the manufacture of metal nails and hinges, textiles, ceramics and leather goods, for example, than upon some of the more glamorous activities which seemed more important in the 1940s and 1950s. The following excerpt from an international Labour Organization paper summarizes the new emphasis:

Since its inception the ILO has provided assistance to small-scale enterprises as part of its general objective to promote economic and social development. More recently, the thrust of this major objective has been sharpened to focus on creating low-capital-cost employment; promoting equity in income-distribution; improving forward and backward linkages between economically, socially and geographically diverse sectors; developing a pool of skilled and semi-skilled workers as a basis for future industrial expansion; providing opportunities for developing, adapting and transferring technological and managerial approaches; increasing savings and investments; improving mobility of scarce capital; exploiting natural resources; promoting special sub-contracting arrangements and improving working conditions and the quality of working life.

The role of the ILO is to provide appropriate inputs for member States to assist them in developing policies, to create and strengthen institutions and to develop programmes designed to promote orderly growth and development of the small enterprise sector. (Meeting of Donor Agencies on Small Scale Enterprise Development, Berlin October 1977)

The new interest in small enterprise in the developing world has many striking points of similarity with the parallel interest in the advanced countries, and many of the institutional and other responses are the same. Banks are criticized for being too cautious in their lending to small firms in Singapore as well as in Southall. The main problems of small firms as perceived by governments in developing countries are curiously similar to those as seen by European governments: lack of finance, training and advice, problems in export marketing, for example. There is also concern about the small number of persons willing to set up new businesses in many developing countries: Malaysia has a National Entrepreneurial Research and Development Association, for example. Even the public and semi-public financial agencies and programmes have a similar structure to their equivalents in the developed world. In fact the recent discovery that heavy government expenditure in inducing large firms to set up branch plants in the poorer regions of the developed countries does little or nothing to promote self-sustaining growth in these regions is of tremendous importance to the developing countries. So too is the related discovery that small firms are many times more likely to spin off employees in new small firms than large firms: this is the most efficient way to get growth going.

CHAPTER 5

Interlude: The Debate

This is the transcript of an imaginary BBC Current Affairs televised discussion on the economic situation some time in 1981. The presenter is a handsome man in his early fifties, he is a professional broadcaster and journalist and rather good at concealing his political views. He tries quite successfully to give the impression that he is too cynical to vote at all. Two of the four panellists are academics. The younger of the two, Wilfred Jones, is very lean, wears a green sports coat with a red tie, has a charming manner and is a professor of economic history at London University. He advises a Labour Minister and is well known for his advocacy of more government intervention. The older academic, Sir John Rushington, was a professor of economics at Oxbridge; he is in his late sixties and looks and is distinguished. He is now on the board of a public corporation and plays no public role in politics. Mrs Godfree is a large and formidable woman who has written and lectured widely upon the virtues of free enterprise. She chairs the board of a large secretarial agency, though in her youth she too taught economics. Ms Zetovsky, who is fragile, very young and pretty, wears a purple wool dress with lots of beads. She works for an American environmental and consumer protection group.

Presenter: (who appears after some stirring music and the symbol of the programme, a series of receding concentric circles. After introductions he begins): This week, unemployment has nearly reached 2½ million. Having fallen since last year, inflation is still in double figures, economic output is stagnant and we have in fact only seen an average annual increase in GDP of about 1.5-2 per cent per annum in the six years since 1974 and much of this is due to North Sea oil. You could say that the UK economy has been in a recession now for six years. It looks very like the 1930s again, only this time we have inflation too. Tonight I should like to concentrate upon the wider implications of all this; let's keep off the short-term outlook and politics and discuss what this five-year experience means for the way we run the economy. Can we eventually see a return to the high levels of growth and employment we had in the 1950s and 1960s on present monetarist policies? Or do we need quite different policies? Sir John, your experience qualifies you best to give us a perspective on this. Do we need to choose between growth and inflation? Should we have continued with the price and incomes controls of the previous labour government? Is capitalism going to survive?

Sir John: I think it has become clear that capitalism is a pretty sturdy animal and has survived many of those who have confidently predicted its collapse, including Marx. The strength of the free market system is, in fact, its responsiveness to changing circumstances. The ability of the system to adapt has undoubtedly been weakened by the monopoly element in wage bargaining and there is in my view a need to exert some control over incomes, especially until expectations of inflation can be brought down. But an incomes policy would have to be more flexible than last time because wage differentials are the main way in which labour is attracted to those activities that the market needs. Of course, incomes in the public sector have to be controlled by the government anyway in some form or another so some form of wage policy is inevitable in a mixed economy. Under the Labour Government price control had already become more flexible because we were controlling margins, not prices as such. This, too, is undesirable because it damps down the signals profits give to encourage resources into expanding activities, and an active competition policy should keep down excessive profits. Nonetheless, although the government is right in keeping a tight rein on the money supply I should like to see another attempt to control or at least to influence incomes. As you said it does look a lot like the 1930s but the world has changed a lot since then. There are appalling difficulties, you know, in introducing radical changes in economic policy in practice. Room for manoeuvre is surprisingly limited − you cannot afford to carry out wild experiments.

Mrs Godfree: But that is exactly what we have been doing! No other country has had any successful experience with our peculiar mix of very high rates of taxation, continually changing interventionist policies, all party support for lame ducks and nationalization of large sectors of industry. We have continued to experiment with the taxation of success and the subsidization of failure and it just doesn't work.

Wilfred Jones: I agree that no other country has our particular mix of policies, but then no other country has our particular mix of problems. Certainly Sweden and other Scandinavian countries have achieved great prosperity with higher rates of taxation than we have. France and Italy have at least as large a public sector as Britain does. Several studies have shown that taxes do not take an exceptionally high proportion of GNP in Britain compared with other countries.

Mrs Godfree: No, but don't forget the tax rate in the UK is high in relation to incomes. We are too poor to pay as much tax as the Germans or Americans, and Sweden is now in bigger trouble than we are ! They've never really recovered from the 1974 recession. As to Italy, well they are hardly a model of economic success and both Italy and France had much lower *marginal* rates of taxation than we did until recently. It is marginal rates that count because they crucially affect incentives: if you know that 90p in the pound of any additional income is going to the taxman, you don't have much incentive to work harder, take risks and raise your income, do you? Personally I don't think that international comparisons are necessarily very instructive, but it is certainly true that those countries which have lower taxes and which have interfered with market forces least have done better than Britain: Germany, Switzerland and the United States, for example. If you take Japan, the most spectacular success of all, it has the smallest public sector and the lowest proportion of tax revenue to GDP of all the industrialized countries.

Wilfred Jones: May I just say that the countries Mrs Godfree mentioned do not have the legacies from the past that Britain has to deal with; they haven't had their manufacturing base eroded, as we have, nor are their economies as concentrated as ours. Mrs Godfree would have us rely on Adam Smith's invisible hand of private interest, but that only worked because many small producers competed with one another: there were no multinational companies in the eighteenth century like the ones that dominate much of international trade and production today. Moreover, the free enterprise system in those days worked at a tremendous social cost: no one is going to agree to a reversal of the social advances we have made. The world is a very different place today, governments have to lead and guide the activities of the market sector, if only because these are producer-dominated, not consumer-dominated as they were in Smith's day.

Presenter: Ms Zetovsky?

Ms Zetovsky: Well, I agree that Western economies have become producer-dominated; they have also become capital and energy intensive, bureaucratic and insensitive to human needs and the realities of our eco-system. A growing number of people in the States and elsewhere reject the alternatives put forward by Mrs Godfree and Wilfred Jones which don't to me seem too different. Market forces, with a lot of help from government, have resulted in a situation in which in most industries a few big corporations control the field, use advertising and financial muscle to keep out newcomers and, in the interests of so-called efficiency and national security, have gotten government to give them handouts, tax reliefs for capital investment and big defence contracts. To be sure, the power of these corporations is now such that government is spending more and more dollars on federal agencies to control them. But these vast bureaucracies are pursuing their own interests and those of the corporations as much as those of the consumer. I guess, he or she is seen increasingly as becoming a nuisance to the smooth operation of the system. Meanwhile social security and education programmes intended to help the disadvantaged are also getting bogged down in bureaucracy and eroding the self-reliance and cramping the self-expression of our people. The Keynesian solution for unemployment, which involves pumping dollars into the system, cannot work because the labour unions and the big corporations together put up the price of labour and pass it on to the consumer with a mark-up for profit. Taxes on these profits are then offset by allowances for more capital intensive methods of production which actually diminish the number of jobs and require more and more energy and more and more damage to the environment. Yet it is labour which is the thing we have in surplus, and capital, energy and our environment which are scarce resources. We need to move towards a more decentralized, less bureaucratic, less energy-intensive, more labour-intensive system in which people can become more self-reliant in small communities and live more in harmony with nature and themselves.

Presenter: What you have said will strike a sympathetic chord with many listeners, but I wonder if it is practicable. Look at the direction technology is moving in and the high standards of living that capital intensive methods of production have made possible. We have all grown accustomed to these things. I'd like us to return to this point later on, but can we now take up your remarks about Keynes. This seems to be central. We have been led to believe that Keynesian policies have been largely responsible for the recovery of economic activity before World War II and the virtually uninterrupted growth and high employment we had up to the early 1970s. Never, we were told, would the slump and unemployment of the 1930s be seen again; economists gave us the impression that Keynes' breakthrough was their profession's greatest achievement. Was it all a mistake and have those in the 1930s who argued against him been proved right? Sir John can you enlighten us? Your earlier remarks suggested that you are something of a Keynesian still.

Sir John: Who was it who said "We are all Keynesians now"?

Ms Zetovsky: Actually it was President Nixon! (Laughter)

Sir John: In a different sense, no doubt from what the unfortunate Mr Nixon meant, we *are* all Keynesians (I speak for economists) because we are all deeply influenced by the techniques and ways of thinking he developed. The whole of what we call macro-economics, that part of our subject which deals with the relationships between aggregates, such as the price level, employment and the balance of payments, indeed the whole idea of national accounts that we have been talking about this evening in our references to GDP, date from Keynes' *General Theory* which appeared in 1936. He also had something to do with the setting up of the International Monetary Fund and many other things.

What he is most remembered for, however, and what Mr Nixon was talking about, were his ideas on the relationship between public expenditure and employment. He argued that in certain circumstances the economy could get 'stuck' permanently at much less than full employment because of an insufficiency of demand and that there was no automatic mechanism that would necessarily ensure recovery. This he saw as the problem in the 1930s. His answer was expenditure on public works which would directly raise employment and through the spending of the wages of the newly employed people would raise demand and output further. We cannot really say that Keynes' ideas got us out of the slump at the time because the Treasury didn't accept them and they were not implemented as such. Budget deficits elsewhere, notably President Roosevelt's New Deal in 1933 where public works created employment, probably did help to restore international demand, but Roosevelt acted before Keynes published his book and wasn't influenced by him. After the War, of course, Keynes' ideas were widely accepted by economists and governments, but we cannot say that in themselves they were responsible for full employment. This would probably have been achieved anyway because of the growth of public expenditure that followed the widespread adoption of collectivist policies on social welfare, public ownership of industry and the like, as well as the increase in investment opportunities which sprang from technical progress, the destruction of much of the capital stock in wartime and so on. It is not at all clear that Keynes won the technical arguments against his protagonists, for example, Pigou in the 1930s. Also some of his detailed arguments were a little fuzzy and have since been the subject of further refinement and debate. I knew Keynes, of course. He was a brilliant man, his ideas were changing and developing all the time. He would not have been at all happy with them now, I'm sure, if he were alive today. In some ways, his *General Theory* was not general at all; it was a special case, the case of the 1930s when there was an exceptional degree of surplus capacity and idle resources virtually throughout the economy. That is not the problem now.

Mrs Godfree: I think you have let Keynes off too lightly, Sir John. His ideas encouraged governments after the war to spend money, something any government is prone to do, and to debase the value of money. They maintained employment in the long post-war boom only at the expense of progressively distorting the structure of the economy through continuous inflation. Over the years successively larger doses of inflation became necessary to maintain employment and in the early 1970s the rate of price increases became unacceptable. We are now faced with the dilemma that if the government pumps in more money, prices will start accelerating again and if it does not, then unemployment will rise. Professor Hayek predicted that this would be the outcome of Keynesian policies when Keynes first put them forward, and he has been proved right. The only answer is to keep the value of money stable by increasing the money supply steadily in line with a realizable output growth. In increasing public expenditure to stimulate employment, governments have been over-expanding the money supply and it is this which is the cause of inflation.

Sir John: Well, we are all monetarists now, too, because it is accepted that control of the money supply is important if only because of its effects upon the exchange rate and that in an open economy like ours, a fall in the exchange rate pushes up prices. But it is not at all clear how increases in the money supply actually feed through into domestic activity and price increases in other ways, except through the rate of interest and investment. This is what the monetarists cannot adequately explain and why I cannot accept that increases in the money supply push up incomes and prices. It seems to me fairly clear that it is the other way round.

Presenter: This is getting a bit technical, Sir John, but yes, what about the wage increases, aren't they the cause of price increases? And don't excessive wage increases create unemployment?

Sir John: Yes, increases in wage costs over and above productivity improvement are rapidly passed on in price increases and if these are sufficiently general and financed by an increase in the money supply, as they normally have to be if there is not to be a liquidity crisis, then the general price level goes up, but there are no real increases in demand and new jobs are not created. An increase in the money supply therefore is the result of wage and price increases, not the cause of it. If the money supply is not increased, then unemployment increases, but inflation as such doesn't seem to be an important cause of unemployment. That is caused by lack of real demand. So, if wages can be kept down, additional employment can be created by more public expenditure. The problem is that full employment encourages wage demands, but unemployment, even at present levels, does not eliminate them. But we shouldn't overemphasize the role of the unions. Their growing power has increasingly weakened the effectiveness of demand management over the whole of the post-war period, but the recent exceptional inflation and recession has other causes. The whole international economic system has suffered from a series of shocks since the early 1970s. The most important have been the breakdown of the pegged exchange rate system from 1971 and the quadrupling of oil prices by OPEC in 1973-74. We can now see in retrospect that the effects of these shocks was compounded by widespread errors in economic policy, notably in the over-expansive monetary policies widely adopted in 1972 and which had been reversed when the oil crisis hit us. The increase in energy prices, which came on top of a boom in raw material prices, resulted in further upward pressures on wages and prices. The transfer of resources to the oil producing countries, who were not able to spend them all on imports, has depressed the level of demand. It is going to take us some time to adjust to all this.

Mrs Godfree: May I add to that: the breakdown of the pegged system of exchange rates itself resulted from the unwillingness of governments to accept the discipline over the control of the money supply that that system requires. Floating exchange rates give governments more freedom to manipulate domestic demand - or so it was thought. The oil crisis, I agree, did create problems, but hampered and constrained as it is, the market system has coped remarkably well with these. The oil producing countries have been forced to see that they cannot control both price and demand. The higher price of oil has stimulated the search for new sources of energy and economy in its use. I also agree that you cannot blame the unions for inflation, this is a monetary phenomenon and is entirely the consequence of governments' failure to control the money supply. If the government does not allow the money supply to increase faster than output then unions *cannot* enforce general wage increases faster than output and there will be no inflation. There will be an increase in unemployment temporarily if the unions insist upon and get excessive wage increases, but the abatement of inflation will help moderate that and the market mechanism will ensure that output will soon start to increase again. All the evidence is that if this system is allowed to work it does have an inherent tendency to full employment. If we are to halt inflation there is no way of avoiding some increase in unemployment. Past inflation, which I repeat is the result of excessive increases in the money supply, has failed to maintain full employment and cannot do so except temporarily at continuously accelerating rates of increase in prices. There is no way of permanently maintaining full employment by pumping money into the system.

Wilfred Jones: I must disagree here. I don't share Mrs Godfree's faith in the market mechanism. Her views of the workings of that mechanism are 200 years out of date. On certain assumptions, and in theory, demand and output might recover after the deflation which she envisages. But one (to take only one) of the implicit assumptions she makes is quite unreal: that there is perfect competition in all markets including factor markets (such as labour). Under perfect competition producers would compete with one another by lowering prices for larger shares in the declining market, declining prices would stimulate demand and the ability of producers to lower prices would simultaneously be reinforced by falling costs and wages. In other words, she assumes downward price flexibility. This was a real enough assumption when there were large numbers of small producers and no trade unions, as in Adam Smith's day, but it is wildly unrealistic now when 50 per cent of the working population is unionized and 100 companies control about the same proportion of manufacturing output. These large companies have the monopolistic power to resist any downward movement in prices and in fact are likely to increase them to maintain their income as demand falls. All this now has an international dimension. These large companies are virtually all multinationals and will resist the depressive effects of devaluation of their home currencies on their own export prices so as to avoid cutting into the sales of their own subsidiaries abroad. Mrs Godfree's view of the market is not only out of date in these ways; it doesn't allow for the effects of actions by governments abroad. What has been happening is that as governments cut their domestic demand in order to reduce imports so as to leave room for the increased value of oil imports, our own scope for export is inevitably reduced. If the UK continues to deflate in the way Mrs Godfree wants, it might set off a round of similar actions by our trading partners. The next stage would be widespread import controls and that would precipitate a really severe world slump. Further cuts in the growth of money supply would certainly increase unemployment very rapidly and no responsible government would do it.

Presenter: I thought you had recently come out in favour of import controls, Professor Jones?

Wilfred Jones: Yes, but selective controls entirely to deal with specific industrial situations where time is needed for adjustment. I had in mind Japanese car imports and imports of footwear and certain textiles from some low-labour cost countries. The problem of competition from low-labour cost countries is yet another one that is not taken into account in Mrs Godfree's view of the world. Nor does she take account of the fact that the capital market isn't working properly. Our de-industrialization results from the diversion of capital from manufacturing investment and into property, services and foreign investment.

Presenter: Mrs Godfree, would you like to come back on that, briefly? I am afraid time is running out.

Mrs Godfree: Thank you. Of course I don't deny that there have been many developments in the structure of the economy but the operation of the laws of the market are not significantly affected by the factors Professor Jones described, except insofar as they result from government interference, such as the establishment of statutory monopolies which are largely, though still not entirely, immune from competition. The workings of the market are responsible for such concentration as has occurred, though it is greatly exaggerated: modern technology requires large-scale organizations in many industries, but competition continues between them. If one large company fails to meet market needs, others will soon step in to exploit the opportunity. In Adam Smith's day competition was largely a local affair between small firms, now it is national and international and the number of producers offering goods to the consumers in any given locality may well be much greater now than it was 200 years ago. Intervention in all its forms has failed, demonstrably. If the market and private enterprise were allowed and encouraged to work, instead of being constrained and discouraged, then new activities would emerge to replace those lost to more efficient competition from abroad. Why should we deny our consumers cheaper imported shoes from developing countries? We should be exporting shoe-making machinery to Brazil as the Germans are doing. As to the failure of the capital market: investors invest in what is profitable. Heaven help us in our old age if pension funds are forced to invest in what Whitehall tells them to! Professor Jones, like a quack eighteenth-century doctor, wants to go on blood-letting when the patient is near the point of death through lack of blood. It is his medicine which is out of date, not mine!

Ms Zetovsky: Yes, the patient certainly is seriously ill and here are we, the doctors, quarrelling around his bedside. I

don't agree with either Mrs Godfree or Professor Jones:
Mrs Godfree, who would apparently allow and encourage
big business to press on towards that inflexible, wasteful,
bureaucratic, capital intensive, environmental nightmare
that her kind of free market will lead us to and Professor
Jones would lead us in the same direction but with, if
anything, less consumer choice and more bureaucracy.
They both talk about GDP as if it measured welfare: it
doesn't do anything of the sort, it omits the supply of
services of housewives and mothers and the more we spend
on bureaucracy and on pollution control the higher it is.
Much of the money we spend and the so-called
contribution made to GDP made by the expenditure and
the output of which it is the counterpart, is necessary
simply to overcome the friction in the system. For
example, it goes on convenience foods, or second cars to
save women the time to go out to work in bureaucracies, or
on holiday homes or travel abroad to unspoiled places to
compensate for the fact that we have ruined our own
environment. It is just crazy how workers are crowded into
big factories making short-lived stuff people don't really
want and which sells only after huge advertising
expenditure. Remember the more spent on advertising the
higher GDP is! The same workers are frustrated and
alienated because they can take no pleasure in
craftmanship and have no influence over the remote
people who influence them, except by joining unions to go
on strike for more money, creating all these inflationary
problems that Sir John isn't sure we have the complete
answer to. The world economy is on a slower growth path
now, so let's stop encouraging big business and
bureaucracy that cannot cope with that and start
encouraging small-scale, community-based activity with
less capital-energy intensive production methods so as to
use the resources we do have in abundance, and release the
creative, innovative energy in people. The efficiency

experts will be surprised how efficient it is! Most modern economics is bunk you know: we have ample proof of that in the mess economists have got us into.

Presenter: Ms Zetovsky, that is a very provocative statement to make in present company. But time will not allow us to hear what the others have to say. Let's conclude provisionally that we have been taking the advice of the wrong economists in the past. Thank you all for a most stimulating discussion. I for one feel that you are *all* right, at least in part, which means I suppose that we have been talking about some of the central dilemmas of our time. I hope we shall be able to follow them up in more detail in future programmes. Good night.

The sound of voices fades away, the stirring music begins again and as the credits rise up from the bottom of the screen, Mrs Godfree and Professor Jones plunge into animated discussion, the Presenter turns to Ms Zetovsky while Sir John looks benignly but thoughtfully at the others. The concentric circles reappear.

CHAPTER 6

The New Economics

The Limitations of Economics

To understand recent developments in the views of
economists on small firms and their role in the economic
system, it is helpful to have some idea of the evolution of
thought on the subject. The layman generally finds the
apparent fascination which most economists have for the
history of economic thought tiresome and irrelevant and
just one more sign of an academic reluctance to get to grips
with reality. In this, as in other respects, economics is
thought to compare unfavourably with the natural and
physical sciences. After all, scientists have produced the
Pill and cures for much disease, their work has made
possible rapid intercontinental air travel, television, the
pocket calculator and many other advances such as nuclear
fission. Even though these advances may have
questionable effects upon human happiness, they have
sufficient human appeal for us to wish to retain them and
all are real and concrete material achievements. Any
layman can produce such a list. It would be a much more
difficult task for him to list the achievements of
economists and probably impossible for him to produce
any which could not be disputed. Even some of the
achievements which have been claimed in the past — for
example, that the Keynesian revolution had abolished

involuntary unemployment – have not been lasting and were arguably illusory.

Economics, like other aspects of social inquiry, is certainly a science in the traditional sense of that term as a department of learning and study. Whether or not economics is a science in the modern sense applied to the natural and physical sciences ('A branch of study which is concerned . . . with a connected body of demonstrated truths . . .' – OED) is more questionable. Economics is much more difficult than the non-social sciences as a field of scientific inquiry, because its subject matter is always changing and because it is not really possible, as it is in the physical sciences, to conduct controlled experiments. Whilst you can measure the resistance of a flow of electricity through a wire in a vacuum at different temperatures and draw conclusions about the effects of temperature changes upon that resistance, you cannot conduct similar experiments in economics. It is not possible to isolate part of an economy in a laboratory in this way. The flow of money through the economy, for example, cannot be measured at all precisely and its effects upon say, the level of prices, will be affected by institutional factors, expectations and all sorts of other internal and external influences which change constantly and can never be held constant.

Some understanding and through that even some control of economic events is possible through the construction and testing of simplified models and upon analysis and deduction based upon past events, but at any given time this understanding and the efficiency of action based upon it is threatened by the constant change that is going on in the economic system. Economists may, therefore, give wrong advice or make poor forecasts, either because they do not fully understand how the system worked in the past or because the system itself is changing so that even a knowledge of how it did work is of limited value. The exercise of economic policy, that is the application of these understandings (or misunderstandings) by government to influence economic events, faces the further difficulty that it takes time to introduce new policies and the system may have changed still further by the time the policies take effect. Matters are complicated still further by the fact that consumers, employees and businessmen can anticipate what governments will do, and take avoiding action which increases the likelihood that shots fired at the moving target of economic events will miss.

The history of economic thought, therefore, should not be seen as an account of an increasingly sophisticated understanding of the workings of *the* economic system, but rather as the development of a series of aerial photographs, some better than others, of how successive systems, or parts of systems, have worked at different times.

Before the emergence of the nation State (and before the emergence of anything resembling modern systematic economic thought) in the modern sense, the source of wealth was primarily thought to be in land and in the control of the people that lived upon it. Between the fifteenth and eighteenth centuries, great emphasis was placed upon international trade as the source of wealth and particularly upon the importance of gold. The Mercantilists believed that the State should intervene in economic affairs to maximize the balance of trade and in doing so were speaking for the interests of the rising class of merchants. Towards the end of the period, a new middle class of manufacturers was emerging and Adam Smith was to show powerfully that competition, not State intervention was the best means for promoting wealth in these new circumstances.

Of course, many features of the workings of the economic system have changed only very slowly over time, just as from the air many of the essential features of the landscape and the history of changes to them are visible. Techniques for economic study have improved, and the accumulation of relevant knowledge has been continuous, but also the economy has become more complex and it is by no means certain that our understanding of the contemporary economy is much greater from the point of view of economic policy than that of economists in, say, the 1930s.

In the inter-war depression, Keynes was arguing that the economy had achieved equilibrium at far below the full employment level and that increased public expenditure was the only practicable way of raising activity and employment. This was opposed by the Treasury establishment, who believed that lower interest rates and real wages would make it profitable for businessmen to invest while public expenditure would simply create an artificial boost to activity that would delay the structural changes (that is the contraction of some industries such as cotton, coal and shipbuilding and the redeployment of their resources elsewhere) that the depression would force through.*

In fact, Keynes' view did not prevail at the time and the economy did recover slowly in the period up to World War II with growth in the new industries such as motor cars and electrical goods contrasting with terrible and prolonged contraction in older industries. With the war, increased public expenditure and the conversion of industry to the war effort soon eliminated unemployment, and high levels of activity were maintained right up to the early 1970s. During this period, Keynesian ideas became the new orthodoxy. However, rapid rates of increases in prices now mean that increased public expenditure can only raise employment without runaway inflation if incomes are

*The history of this period and the Keynesian-monetarist controversy are dealt with simply but in more detail elsewhere in Bannock 1975.

tightly controlled and this seems to be impracticable in a democracy, even if the side effects upon differentials and structural change could be mitigated.

We cannot know what would have happened had Keynes' views been accepted in the 1930s, but we do know that things are different now with the much greater role of the State in the economy, a more concentrated industrial structure, stronger trades unions and a changed world abroad. The prevailing view now is that of the monetarists who believe that given time, provided the growth in the money supply is controlled and steadied, inflation will decline and the economy will sort itself out. This is, in effect, a reversion to the neo-classical view of the 1930s (though inflation was not then the problem) but there is an even greater realization now of the difficulties of economic policy and implementation. Economists and politicians alike are increasingly aware that there is no simple solution, no technical device which can be applied in isolation to solve economic problems. Crude monetarism, like crude Keynesianism before it, will probably, in time, wilt under the complexities of influencing economic change. We still do not really know how the money and 'real' economies work and interrelate; what we are beginning to appreciate is that whatever technical approach we adopt, there is no dodging the concrete issues: the creation and use of resources; the real limits to the volume of public expenditure; structural change and individual motivation and productivity. To this extent, the philosopher's stone appeal of macro-economics, in either its Keynesian or monetarist manifestations, has collapsed and attention will increasingly turn towards these underlying matters and towards institutional economics in which another great economist, Joseph Schumpeter, opened up new, but subsequently neglected, avenues of inquiry in the 1940s.

Economists and Small Business

This is the background against which the new interest in small firms needs to be seen. As mentioned in chapter 1, political interest in small firms has risen with concern about unemployment. Since small firms are labour intensive the promotion of small firms should promote job creation. Another factor has been the growth in the power of the small firm lobby which though still weak and fragmented, has drawn the attention of politicians to the large number of votes which the small business sector still commands. Real interest in small firms, though, has had to wait upon events. The Committee of Inquiry on Small Firms reported in 1971 to an indifferent public: were it to report today, it would get different treatment. In the meantime, quite a lot of research has been carried out by economists which suggests that small business is even more important to economic development than the Bolton Committee was able to show.

The history of economic thought on the place of small firms in the industrial structure is fairly straightforward, at least until the 1940s. The position of the classical economists was clearly expressed by J. S. Mill, who wrote in his *Principles of Political Economy* (1848):

> . . . of large establishments generally, when compared with small ones, whenever competition is free its results will show whether individual or joint stock agency is best adapted to the particular case, since that which is most efficient and most economical will always, in the end, succeed in underselling the other.

In other words, provided firms are not monopolists, market forces will ensure that they operate at the optimum scale; industrial structure will be determined by competition. At the time, virtually all manufacturing activity was conducted by owner-managed businesses, although there were some very large joint stock companies (the equivalent of modern quoted companies) in overseas trading, public utilities and transport. In fact Mill saw clearly that increasing returns to scale arising from the division of labour and the use of capital equipment would lead to the concentration of many industries into fewer, larger firms, but this was a problem for the future. Interestingly he anticipated J. K. Galbraith a century later in arguing that trades unions would, and should, emerge to countervail the increasing power of large employers.

Marx, after Mill, foresaw increasing concentration as part of the whole process by which capitalism would evolve into socialism, but the accompanying deterioration in the earnings of workers and the violent class struggle and revolution which he envisaged did not materialize outside Russia. The general availability of limited liability for private companies in the 1850s, the development of the capital market and the ever increasing capital required for new methods of production led to the emergence of larger and larger industrial companies both before and after the First World War. True monopolies, where it was understood that there was little competitive check on behaviour, remained rare and mainly confined to statutory monopolies. Economists in the 1930s recognized that concentration had increased and developed a theory of imperfect competition. This enabled them to handle the fact that in many industries, though not monopolies, where one firm controlled the bulk of sales, a large proportion of output was now controlled by a few firms. The general belief was that, although output was lower and prices higher than under perfect competition, these prices were not necessarily higher than under any practical alternative: where the optimum scale of product was large in relation to the size of the market, prices might still in these circumstances be lower than in conditions where large numbers of firms were working at below the optimum scale. Even where there was doubt about this, the prevailing view in Britain was that State intervention in the determination of output and prices was preferable to any attempt to restore competition. Modern technology required large scale and this inevitably meant fewer and larger firms.

After World War II attitudes towards large firms became more positive and remained so until the end of the 1960s. Attention focused upon the role of large firms in innovation. In an enormously influential book the American economist Schumpeter (1943) argued that:

> . . . it is not sufficient to argue that because perfect competition is impossible under modern conditions − or because it always has been impossible − the large-scale establishment or unit of control must be accepted as a necessary evil inseparable from the economic progress which it is prevented from sabotaging by the forces inherent in its productive apparatus. What we have got to accept is that it has come to be the most powerful engine in that progress and in particular of the long-run expansion of total output, not only in spite of, but to a considerable extent through, this strategy which looks so restrictive when viewed in the individual case and from the individual point of time.

For Schumpeter price competition between firms in the static sense of traditional competitive theory was relatively unimportant: what were important were the 'gales of creative destruction' which swept away products, processes and forms of organization and replaced them with new ones:

> In the case of retail trade, the competition that

matters arises, not from additional shops of the same type, but from the department store, the chain store, the mail order house and the supermarket which are bound to destroy those pyramids sooner or later.

In industrial development the process of innovation in large firms was, according to Schumpeter, 'being reduced to routine' in which teams of specialists 'turn out what is required and make it work in predictable ways'. The higher profits under monopolistic (as compared with perfect) competition were an important condition for technical progress. Attempts by governments to make large firms behave as they would under perfect competition would be counter-productive: the system had to be allowed to run its course so as to permit revolution from within.

These powerful ideas took their grip upon the minds of many economists so that they became the new orthodoxy throughout the 1950s and 1960s. They were buttressed by the lack of any clear evidence that the market structure of the advanced economies had actually changed much further towards concentration. Whilst it was obvious that in many industries, small and medium-sized companies were being absorbed into larger units, the growth of international trade and the multinational corporations meant that large domestic producers were increasingly facing competition from abroad. It was argued that within national boundaries small local markets, once dominated by small local suppliers, were being broken up by the intrusion of national producers and the largest companies were also continually diversifying out of their traditional product lines and into those of their competitors. Thus, although firms were getting larger, market concentration, that is to say the share of the top three or four sellers, was not necessarily increasing. Moreover, it was continually pointed out that the vast majority of firms were still small in most industries.

What might be called the Schumpeterian view that big is not only inevitable but best, seemed impregnable and was apparently continually being reinforced by developments in retailing, where large supermarkets were keeping prices down, in supertankers which were cutting the costs of oil transport and in manufacturing where the optimum scale of production in motor manufacture, for example, seemed to keep on rising. The enormous sums for research and development in computers, nuclear power and aviation all seemed to be pointing to the rapid disappearance of any significant role for small firms in modern economic development. Moreover, and this was the most convincing justification of all, the system was working well: the three decades, ending in the early 1970s, saw the most rapid and sustained period of economic growth since the nineteenth century.

Just as rising inflation and other problems emerged to threaten the post-war boom in the 1960s, so too was a growing volume of empirical economic research calling into question the contemporary relevance of much of the Schumpeterian view on industrial structure and economic development.

Market and Aggregate Concentration

First it began to be clear that changes *were* going on in market concentration, not in the United States, where there appeared to have been little change since the rush of mergers and amalgamations at the end of the nineteenth century, but in most other developed countries. In the UK, an early study by Evely and Little found that, in 41 industries for which comparisons were valid over the period 1935-51, concentration had increased in twice as many sectors as it had fallen. Later studies showed a still faster rate of increase in seller concentration and one, by

Hart, Utton and Walshe, indicated that, in those industries where concentration had increased, mergers accounted for half of the change. An answer to a Parliamentary question in 1970 contained the surprising statistic that one firm had 50 per cent or more of the market in 156 product areas.

Of course, evidence of increasing seller concentration was quite consistent with the Schumpeterian thesis and the lack of any increase in the United States was simply evidence that further concentration there was unnecessary to achieve economies of scale given the enormous size of its domestic market. In several European countries, including the UK, government policy had favoured concentration to correct an 'excessively' fragmented industrial structure, so that the emergence of larger firms was a sign that this policy was working. Nonetheless, an increase in seller concentration was disturbing for those who believed that the industrial structure was self-policing and particularly for those who had argued that overall it could not happen.

New evidence on trends in overall or aggregate concentration as measured by the share of the 100 largest enterprises in output was even more disturbing. After declining in the 1930s and 1940s aggregate concentration now seemed to be increasing everywhere and in some countries, including Britain, at an accelerating rate. As mentioned in chapter 1, the share of the 100 largest companies, in UK net output, rose from 16 per cent in 1909 to around 40 per cent in 1970. In the US, according to Prais, the comparable figures were 22 and 33 per cent over the same period. Now these trends are also consistent with the Schumpeterian thesis, but they did raise the question of where the process, if it continued, would lead. Whilst some economists pointed out that aggregate concentration has no necessary implications for monopoly (which is measured by seller concentration) ultimately increased aggregate concentration would eventually lead to monopoly in individual markets. More recently, J. D.

Gribbin has shown that high levels of aggregate concentration and monopoly in the traditional sense do go together. Of the 100 largest companies in the UK, approximately half have two or more statutory monopolies (market shares for defined product groups exceeding 25 per cent) and twenty companies have five or more monopolies. Finally Hannah and Kay (1977) have now produced evidence that virtually all of the increase in concentration that occurred between 1957 and 1973 was the result of mergers between existing companies, not internal growth.

It may seem surprising that there can be any doubt about the degree of concentration. Changes in market concentration are not, in fact, easily measured for technical reasons and because the necessary data are available only at long intervals and are rarely fully comparable over long periods of time. (Changes over a short period may have no significance.) Aggregate concentration presents fewer difficulties, but it is interesting that in Britain no one bothered to update estimates made by Prais in the middle 1950s until the late 1960s. In the US, Berle and Means made estimates of aggregate concentration in the 1930s, but these too were not extended until several decades later.

Small Firms and Innovation

Second, and this time more directly damaging to the Schumpeterian view, evidence was accumulating that, despite the apparently overwhelming advantages of large firms, small firms continued to play an important role in invention and innovation. Jewkes, Sawers and Stillerman (1959) were probably the first to produce systematic data on this subject. They showed that, of some 70 post-1900 inventions, more than half were made by men working on their own, or with private help, for example, Cockerall with the hovercraft, and Zuse, Eckert, Mauchly and Von Neumann with the perfecting of the computer. The remainder were split between large and small companies, government bodies and other sources. The role of individuals and small companies was less striking in innovation, that is, in the commercialization of new ideas, than in invention, but it was and is still important.

More recent studies have removed all doubt, confirming that small firms continue to play an important role in innovation. Moreoever, it has been suggested that the inherent limitations in the type of research carried out by these studies may greatly understate the contribution of small firms. Research inevitably has to focus upon radical technical innovation, rather than upon the countless minor advances in products and processes or in marketing and organization, which play such a vital role in economic growth. If the newly identified contribution by small firms, to employment growth, discussed below, is any indication of their contribution to innovation – and there are good reasons for thinking that it is – then this would support the view that this contribution has been understated in the past. To take Schumpeter's own examples from retailing, mail order was pioneered by small firms even if later Sears Roebuck and the great British catalogue mail order houses were to be build large businesses upon it. Practical observation, as well as at least one systematic study, support the view that almost all firms, large and small, are based on some kind of innovation. Certainly virtually all large firms started off as a small firm with an innovation and grew on the basis of it.

Studies also suggest that research and development work is more productive in small firms than in large. In other words, small firms tend to be more efficient users of skilled manpower and R&D equipment. These things cannot be measured with any precision since innovations are not equally important, but all the evidence is that the share of small firms in the number of innovations greatly exceeds their share in R&D expenditure. It may be objected that large firms, because of their greater financial and other resources, concentrate upon capital intensive innovation, and this is undoubtedly true, but it is also probable that the concentration of financial resources in large firms has imparted a capital intensive bias in technological development. Technological development is not a neutral, autonomous thing: advances will be made in those directions in which there is the greatest need and profit and where the greatest effort is applied. It seems highly likely that because the greater part of resources are devoted to large-scale technology, this is the type of technology which will emerge. Thus, if society's resources are channelled mainly to large firms, and large firms are needed to exploit large-scale technology, concentration will be reinforced by technological development.

Production and Financial Economies of Scale

However, whether this is so or not, a third new development in economic research has been just as damaging to the Schumpeterian thesis as the establishment of the fact that large firms are not the sources of most innovation. It is now clear that economies of scale and the requirement for large plants cannot explain the growth in aggregate concentration or the decline in the quantitative importance of small firms. The nature of the evidence is quite simple, though not immediately obvious. If aggregate concentration were increasing because of an increase in the size of plant, then the share of the largest plants or establishments in total output would also be increasing. But S. J. Prais (1976) found that this has not happened. He calculated that the share of the 100 largest UK manufacturing *establishments* remained at about 11 per cent between 1930 and 1968, while that of the 100 largest *enterprises* rose from something around 22 per cent to 41 per cent over the same period. This was a conclusion of great importance, since it meant that the increase in aggregate concentration was not the result of firms building larger and larger plants, but of building or acquiring more plants. In fact, he also calculated that the average number of plants owned by these enterprises rose from 27 in 1958 to 72 in 1972, and that average employment in these plants actually declined sharply over the period. This was not because the largest firms were building smaller plants, but because they were acquiring small plants by buying up small firms. 17 per cent of all establishments employing 200 or fewer persons were owned by large enterprises in 1968 compared with 12 per cent in 1958, while the total number of small establishments fell from 80,000 to 70,000 over the same period.

Prais' work, therefore, showed clearly that technological economies of scale at the plant level could not explain increasing concentration. It was true, as he showed, that the average scale of production was increasing because average plant sizes were increasing: in other words even 'small' plants were getting larger, but this did not account for the fact that the largest enterprises were outstripping the rest. Various economies of management of multi-plant operation could, of course, be identified: for example, in advertising and communications, but these were not sufficiently important in themselves to explain increased concentration. Much more important were financial factors.

In brief, the large multi-plant enterprise can obtain

finance more cheaply, and what is more important, can obtain it more easily than the small single plant enterprise. For bank overdrafts, the blue chip company is likely to pay 3 percentage points or more less than an independent small firm and in many cases the director of that firm will be asked to give personal guarantees or other collateral. For other types of finance, the relative disadvantage of the small firm is much greater. It cannot obtain loans or equity capital from the stock market and must rely upon borrowings from the directors or other private sources. The incidence of higher taxation which has been associated with the increased role of government over the past 100 years has made it more difficult for private individuals to accumulate funds for investment in their own businesses and it has also introduced a strong bias into the allocation of institutional funds towards large firms.

Tax reliefs for savings in insurance and pension funds have channelled the savings of all sectors of the population increasingly into large financial institutions. These institutions do not find it economic to parcel out this money into the small amounts required by small firms, but invest the bulk of it in government securities, the equity and loan stock of quoted companies and property. The tax system again works to favour the acquisition of small companies by large in that whilst the individual owners of small firms pay income tax on any drawings they may make (or corporation tax on any profits they may retain in the business) if they sell their company to a large firm, they will pay tax on the proceeds only at the typically much lower capital gains rate. Moreover, if they are inheriting the business, part of the equity may have to be sold in order to raise the money to pay capital transfer tax and normally the only buyer will be a large firm or a financial institution. At the same time, large firms can borrow money at fixed interest, which is deductible for corporation tax, in order to pay for the acquisition of smaller firms.

Other financial factors have encouraged concentration. Inflation has reduced the real burden of borrowings while the separation of ownership from control in large firms has increased their vulnerability to take-over. Whereas in the typical small firm the management owns the business, the board of directors of one of the 100 largest companies typically controls only about 0.5 per cent of the equity. This means that, as the process of concentration leads to the dilution of management control, so the vulnerability of firms to take-over bids increases and the process of concentration becomes self-reinforcing.

We find, therefore, that whilst concentration is increasing, there is no evidence that this is the result either of an overwhelming advantage which large firms have in innovation (which the Schumpeterian thesis would have us believe) or of the growth of technological economies of scale (which in the past many economists have argued is the principal social justification for concentration).

Is it possible then that the decline of small enterprise is justified by the financial economies which are undoubtedly enjoyed by large firms? The answer to this must be 'no' since the financial advantages of large firms do not mainly represent significant savings in real resources (though there must be some), but simply a transfer of resources to the shareholders in large firms or the consumer of their products from the rest of the economy. This can be seen clearly to apply to the tax savings that arise from the deduction of loan interest from corporation tax and to the savings that arise from the reduction in the real burden of borrowing from inflation. These represent transfers from the taxpayer generally, and the providers of finance respectively. Where a large firm borrows from a bank more cheaply than a small firm, the bank is subsidizing the large firm from the higher interest paid by small firms or other borrowers: there is no evidence that the net costs of lending to small firms *as a group*, even allowing for risk and administrative costs, is as much as the interest rate differential indicates. It should be remembered that even the administrative savings are probably, or at least partly, illusory since where a large firm borrows a large sum from a bank and parcels it out amongst its subsidiaries, it is bearing administrative costs which the bank would bear if it made separate loans to these subsidiaries.

The use of cheap finance does not therefore *in itself* lead to significant savings in real resources which are represented by the labour, materials and capital equipment used in the process of production. Where, because it is able to raise the necessary finance or raise it more cheaply, the subsidiary of a large firm uses more capital equipment than a small firm and is able to undersell its smaller rival as a result, this is a consequence of an imperfection in the capital market (or a deficiency in the management of the small firm) not of any greater efficiency in the use of resources by the large firm. These matters are not straightforward and there are further complications when the ability of large firms to borrow abroad and other factors are taken into account. In fact, it can be shown that in most cases differences in the cost of borrowings are not very important in determining the relative competitiveness of small and large firms in practice; what is more important is that small firms may not be able to borrow at all and cannot therefore get themselves in a position to compete.

Small Firms and Economic Develoment

Fourth, a great deal of other recent empirical research has buttressed the case against the view that contemporary economic development depends and will continue to depend almost entirely upon large firms. (No one has ever denied that small firms were the crucial engine of change and development during the industrial revolution; the argument under criticism here is that under modern conditions there is no longer an important role for the smaller firm.) Comparative studies of the industrial structure of economies in different countries, as we have seen, do not suggest any correlation between the importance of large firms and the level of output, or the rate of economic growth. At a micro-economic level, careful studies by Newbould, Singh, Meeks and others have shown that mergers and acquisitions, which have contributed substantially to increased concentration, have had disappointing effects upon the financial performance of the participating firms. Other studies show that profitability tends to be higher in concentrated than in fragmented industries which suggests that concentration is profitable, even if it may not be socially beneficial, although too much should not be made of that, for comparisons of returns on assets are full of pitfalls.

Various attempts have been made to compare the profitability of small with large firms in the belief that this might throw light upon their relative efficiency, but these comparisons are not meaningful. Not only should the degree of competition be allowed for and other factors such as the inclusion of some return on capital in directors' renumeration among small firms, but comparisons of return on capital (profitability) are only valid measures of the efficient use of resources where inputs of capital and labour are similar. Although most studies suggest that small firms are more profitable than large, it is also found that value added per employee is higher in large firms than in small. All such studies show that small firms get a better return on capital and a worse return on labour, which simply reflects the well known fact that they are more labour intensive than large firms.

Small Firms and Employment

Fifth and finally, very recent research on the contribution of firms of different sizes to the growth of employment in different countries has shown that small firms have accounted for a major proportion of long-term gains in jobs, while the largest firms have been shedding labour. Much interest has been aroused by the publication from 1978 onwards of some research by David Birch of MIT into the components of employment change in the United States (Birch 1979). His frequently quoted result that: 'small firms (those with 20 or fewer employees) generated 66 per cent of all new jobs in the US' in the period 1969-76 was clearly, if valid, of tremendous importance. It seemed that here, at last, was irrefutable evidence of the vital role of small firms in the economy that would justify a major shift in public policy towards the promotion of small business. (Small firms in this study are defined to include subsidiaries and branches of larger enterprises; independents employing 20 or fewer employees accounted for 51.8 per cent of new jobs.)

However, when the details of Birch's research were studied it became clear that most of the new jobs had been generated in the service sector (in which small firms predominate anyway) and not in manufacturing, which is the sector that most politicians (and most economists) are most concerned with. There is now some confusion about the significance of Birch's results for economic policy.

The first point to make is that *all* statistics on very small firms are suspect, but for what they are worth it is possible to see from ordinary census statistics that the overall reduction of employment which has taken place in Britain (and in the US) during the last decade has been concentrated entirely among medium and large firms. Table 6.1 shows that employment in UK firms with less than 100 persons increased in the period 1973-76. In the

TABLE 6.1: Net employment change in manufacturing in the United Kingdom (1973-76) and the United States (1967-72) by size of firm

Number of employees in individual firms	Total employed ('000)		
	United Kingdom 1973	1976	Net change
1-99	1,108.6	1,189.4	+ 80.8
100-199	396.9	386.9	− 10.0'
200 and over	5,762.9	5,394.9	− 368.0'
TOTAL	7,268.4	6,971.2	− 297.2
	United States 1967	1972	Net change
under 19	1,042.3	1,114.2	+ 71.9
20-99	3,276.4	3,355.7	+ 79.3
100-249	3,069.2	3,233.4	+ 164.2
250 and over	11,103.8	10.331.1	− 772.7
TOTAL	18,492.0	18,034.4	− 457.6

SOURCE: UK Reports on the Census of Production (enterprises);
US Census of Manufactures (establishments).

US, similar statistics show that employment increased in establishments employing under 250. (These figures cover different periods but are the latest available in each case.) A similar pattern is to be found in Japanese census figures.

There are several difficulties in drawing conclusions from figures of these kinds, although the simple one that small firms are still creating jobs while big firms are shedding them is broadly correct. It must be understood, however, that within each of the employment size classes indicated, some firms are expanding their employment while others are contracting, and that between the dates shown some firms will have gone out of business while others will have moved up or down into different size classes. A further problem is that you will get different results according to the time period you choose for the comparison. Between 1954 and 1972, for example, figures from the same source show that total employment in firms with less than 20 employees *declined* in the United States even though total employment in manufacturing rose during that period. In the UK in particular, the increase in small firm employment dates from the early 1970s, reversing a long period of decline. These are some of the reasons why Birch, following the pioneering work of Graham Gudgin and others, attempted a different approach: that of comparing the contribution of firms of different sizes to net employment change using a data file of employment in individual firms at different dates.

Birch has, in fact, been criticized by Gudgin (who first clearly established the importance of small firms in employment change) for exaggerating the role of the smallest firms in job creation by failing to disaggregate his results between manufacturing and non-manufacturing (Fothergill and Gudgin 1979). Gudgin thinks job creation in manufacturing is much more important because of its importance in foreign trade and because the creation of wealth in manufacturing is a prior condition for increased employment in services. Gudgin and his co-authors in another study (Gudgin, Brunskill and Fothergill 1979) seem not to be sympathetic to small firms on other grounds: '. . . the desirability of encouraging new firms depends a great deal on longer term political goals. It is worth remembering, for example, that small firms (and most new firms are small) pay lower wages on average, and

TABLE 6.2 Net employment change, United States manufacturing, 1969-76, by size and status of enterprise (figures in thousands)

	Size in numbers of employees					
	0-20	21-50	51-100	101-500	501+	TOTAL
Independent firms (single establishment)	+355	-38	-116	-217	-55	-70
Headquarters and branches of multi-plant firms	+139	+83	+41	-43	-247	-28
Partnerships and subsidiaries	+49	+48	+34	+6	-190	-52
TOTAL	+543	+93	-41	-254	-492	-150

SOURCE: *The Job Generation Process*, David L. Birch, MIT, 1979.

offer fewer fringe benefits to their employees . . .'
However, even in manufacturing, Birch's data (table 6.2),
Gudgin's own figures for the East Midlands and the crude
statistics in table 6.1 all show that smaller firms as a group
are responsible for net increases in employment while
larger firms have been responsible for a net *loss* of jobs.
These data suggest, incidentally, that small firms in Britain
run out of steam at some point below 100 employees while
in the US job losses set in after 250 employees, although it
is difficult to draw any clear conclusions.

It can be seen from table 6.1, that firms with less than
100 employees account for only a small part of total
employment and the 81,000 employment increase in these
firms between 1973 and 1976 was only about 1 per cent of
total manufacturing employment. Because of this,
Gudgin's argument goes, these firms cannot be relied upon
to have much effect upon total employment in the short
run. However it is obvious that the contribution of these
firms in this period is in a different direction to that of
large firms as a group and quite large in relation to the
total employment change. However, Gudgin seems quite
justified in emphasizing (as has been done in this book)
that small firms offer no quick panacea to the economic
problem.

In all these studies, it has been shown that firm
migration has been of little importance in regional
employment growth; the main factor has been the setting
up of new firms. Gudgin has shown that the origins of
small firms are highly localized and that small businesses
breed and interrelate with each other in an organic fashion.
This is because people who work in small firms are much
more likely to set up a business of their own than
employees in large firms. Regions which have no source of
employment other than the branch plants of large
companies, therefore, will experience few employment
gains unless the activities of those plants happen to be in

growth industries; few new activities are likely to be generated in them. This is why some of the areas dominated by large firms in the shipbuilding, steel and other declining industries are economic deserts which have remained unaffected by the attempts by successive governments to encourage other large firms to set up branch plants in them. Thus, much of regional policy as well as the broader policies to promote rationalization and mergers have proved ineffective, based as these policies were on an incomplete understanding of the roots of industrial expansion. It is not even true, as was once thought, that small firms are not significant in export trade. In the service trades small hotels and restaurants serving tourists as well as commodity brokers and others contribute to 'invisible' exports though, of course, many small firms cannot export. In manufacturing it seems that small firms export about the same proportion of their output, on average, as large firms. According to a survey of companies carried out by the Department of Trade in 1973, firms with a turnover of less than £10 million exported 14.5 per cent of turnover while firms with a turnover of over £250 million exported only 10 per cent. (Quoted in Hannah and Kay 1977.)

The implications of all this research have not yet been fully digested by economists and further changes are probably underway that may leave our understanding trailing behind events. It should not be thought that Schumpeter, whose thesis has been taken as the focal point for criticism, was necessarily wrong at the time he was writing. In the 1930s, 1940s and 1950s, large monopolistic firms may well have been the engines of economic progress in some sense that is not our concern here. He was certainly right and very farsighted in focusing upon the dynamic as against the static aspects of the competitive process. But we cannot look to large firms alone now as the engine of development and it was an error to do so in the past.

Interactions between Small and Large Firms

Although from time to time changing problems and opportunities as well as political exigencies may dictate changes in emphasis in government policy towards industrial structure, we should not lose sight of the interrelated nature of this structure. Both large and small firms have vital roles to play in both the static and the dynamic workings of the advanced economy.

Some activities do, by their very nature, require large amounts of capital, or people: aerospace manufacture, oil exploration, development and distribution are two examples. There is probably no way in which these activities can be organized on a small scale if they are to be carried out at all. Practically everything else, if we are to speak broadly, can be and is conducted on both a small and a large scale, each scale catering for different kinds of market requirement: agriculture, hotels and catering, retailing, publishing, motor manufacture, electronics and construction are examples in which a few large and many small firms co-exist. Of course, within these broad categories some things are more suited to small-scale activity than others – retailing in remote rural areas, for example – and certain categories are so suitable for the small firm that large firms can only rarely compete – highly specialized low volume manufacturing or fashion goods, for example. Even where a large firm requires inputs of these kinds, it may choose to subcontract or buy in from small firms rather than manufacture itself. At the other end of the scale, there are very few broad types of activity that can only be carried out on a small scale: these are mainly in the services where a high level of individual personal commitment and creativity is required – authorship and landscape gardening are examples.

Now the balance of advantage between small and large-scale operations is changing all the time with technology, tastes and factor costs. Changing tastes and rising transport costs appear to be causing a decline in the relative advantage of large-scale bread manufacture in the UK, for example, so that not only is the small baker finding an increasing market but supermarkets are installing mini-bakeries. A quickening pace of change and the free availability of low cost components has probably increased the relative advantage of small-scale manufacture for some electronics goods.

Interactions between small and large firms in the process of economic growth, however, are also creating new opportunities for both large and small-scale activity and these must also be understood if we are to avoid damaging shifts of policy which distort the balance between the two. As large firms grow by investing in more and more capital-intensive methods of production they may not, and indeed have not, created much new employment. But the increased value added per employee which this investment makes possible raises output and incomes and these higher incomes create new opportunities for small firms. The growth of new firms in the service industries, for example, is traceable to the increased output per head among large firms in the manufacturing sector. Again as large firms grow, their activities become more complex and it becomes economic to spin off some new specialized work to small subcontractors and suppliers. It would be misleading therefore to interpret the results of recent research on job creation by small firms as a denial of the role of large firms in this process.

These interactions work both ways. New small firms are set up to exploit opportunities for new products and services which technical development and higher incomes create; sometimes innovation is subcontracted by large firms to small (see p.31-2). Of course, large firms also innovate, but many opportunities exist at the outset only on a small scale and the small firm is an ideal vehicle for testing them out: if the enterprise succeeds, then as the market grows, the idea, or perhaps the whole firm exploiting it, may later be taken up by a large firm for mass commercialization. If it fails, there is little economic or social dislocation and the resources of the small firm can be more or less smoothly absorbed elsewhere.

There is no way, for the moment at least, in which the complexities in this flux and change of costs and opportunities can be measured to enable us to determine at any given time, what is the optimal structure of firms of different sizes. Nor, it seems, can we assume that market forces alone, given the influence of monopoly and government actions upon the outcome, will operate to determine that optimum for us. However, given the rapidly increasing accumulation of evidence that attitudes to concentration have been too permissive for too long, there is now an overwhelming, and indeed generally accepted, presumption that some shift in policies in favour of smaller-scale enterprises is necessary.

CHAPTER 7

New Policies

Should We Discriminate in Favour of Small Firms?

It is now nearly a decade since the Bolton Committee put the small business problem firmly on the table in Britain. Some useful things have been done by successive governments in this period: some tax reliefs have been granted; more recently, higher rates of income tax have been cut; and attempts have been made to improve the availability of information and to reduce paperwork for small firms. In the light of the diagnosis of the problem put forward in this book, however, these measures have been very inadequate. If there has been an improvement in the rate of new firm formation recently, it is less the result of deliberate action by government than of the deterioration in the economic climate, which has forced more people to start up on their own as the only available chance of improving their financial circumstances. If this is so (and both the extent of the recovery in new firm formation and its causes are uncertain) then, although this is a propitious time to give a strong policy push, there are no grounds for complacency about the need for quite radical measures.

Although the Bolton Committee identified most of the issues raised in this book (including the distortion of capital markets arising from the effects of the tax system and the role of small firms in innovation and growth) its recommendations fell short of what was required for two main reasons. In the first place, like the Wilson Committee which followed it, the Committee of Inquiry on Small Firms interpreted its terms of reference as excluding a detailed consideration of the 'general shape' of the tax system. Since taxation is one of the most, if not the most important issue, this limitation was bound to weaken the effectiveness of any recommendations made.

In the second place the Bolton Committee was much concerned to avoid 'positive discrimination' in favour of small firms. It recognized that there were many factors which distort competition between large and small firms and recommended that as far as possible these should be removed but balked from discrimination in favour of 'a group whose members are certainly not, as a group among the less fortunate and underprivileged, and who include some of the more wealthy people in the country . . . unless the need for it can be proved beyond all reasonable doubt'. The Committee's Report continued:

> This is not to say that positive discrimination in favour of small firms should be renounced on principle and for all time . . . If later statistics showed an acceleration of the rate of decline − then it will be necessary to consider what action the Government should take to support the sector.

In retrospect it now seems that it may have been a mistake for the Committee to assume that any particular rate of decline in the number of small firms and their share in economic activity was a danger signal for the health of the economy, just as the present signs of a reversal of that trend do not mean that the problem has disappeared. The Committee appreciated that there was no way in which the optimum size of the small firms sector could be calculated and yet assumed that if the rate of decline accelerated that would justify intervention. Given the new evidence that has appeared since 1971 on the role of small firms in economic development and on economic concentration, it is now more plausible to argue that a widespread decline in the small firm sector would sooner or later affect the rate of economic growth and probably had already done so at the time of the Report. Of course, in many of the most important issues in economics, it is not possible to prove anything beyond all reasonable doubt and this is one of them. However, most new initiatives in economic policy in Britain since World War II have been founded on a weaker empirical and theoretical basis than the proposals made in this book.

Furthermore, if the analysis of the problem presented here is correct, what is required is not so much positive discrimination in favour of small firms, in the sense of interference with market forces — though given the magnitude of the task some temporary discrimination probably is desirable — as a radical attempt to ensure freer competition so as to allow market forces to work properly. The argument is that distortions have arisen in both factor markets and final and intermediate markets that have depressed the size of the small firm sector below the optimum. These distortions, like the decline of small business, are not restricted to Britain although most are greater in Britain than elsewhere and this may explain to some extent why the decline has been correspondingly greater here than elsewhere.

The argument that discrimination between firms of different sizes by governments is necessarily wrong because it leads to a distortion of market forces is the reverse of the truth. To treat small firms in the same way as large is usually, in fact, to discriminate against them. Differences in the size of the businesses carry with them differences in capacity to cope with government taxation and regulation in all its aspects. There are, in fact, economies of scale in dealing with government legislation: a small firm can spread the cost of meeting government regulation and paperwork over a smaller sales turnover than a large firm. Motivations are also different and legislation to solve problems arising in large firms is irrelevant as well as burdensome to small firms. Much of company law is concerned with the protection of the shareholder from deprivation by the management, but in a small firm the shareholder and the management are usually the same people. To give another example, large firms and particularly property companies, may find it profitable to leave office buildings empty so that most local authorities levy rates on vacant premises to discourage this, a practice which places an additional burden on small firms with long leases moving from one set of premises to another and unable immediately to relet their old offices.

Table 7.1 lists the main problem areas of small firms − as seen both by observers and small firm proprietors themselves − together with an additional one, the supply of new entrepreneurs, which troubles only the observers since most businessmen are not worried about lack of new competition. The rest of this chapter discusses the broad lines of an approach to the solution of these problems in Britain (which is, of course, relevant in most respects in all countries) and concludes with a discussion of some institutional changes which may be necessary if the solutions are to be effective. It is emphasized that what are put forward here are not comprehensive or fully researched proposals, but examples only of the direction in which action should be taken if the problems discussed in this book are to be tackled seriously. Many of the proposals made would require action at EEC as well as UK government level since they run counter to present intentions on tax and company law harmonization.

TABLE 7.1: Small Firm Problems and their Solution

Problem area	Diagnosis	Action needed on:
Supply of entrepreneurs	Social and economic bias in favour of employment	Social security system Education Tax system
Lack of capital	Distortions in capital market	Tax system Subsidized lending Monopoly policy Credit guarantees
Labour shortages	Imperfections in labour market	Social security system Social environment Housing policy Training and education Monopoly policy
Lack of premises	Imperfections in market	Urban redevelopment Planning regulations Infrastructure investment Tax system
Bureaucracy	Growth of government	Simplification, exemption, changes in local taxation and the organization of central and local government
Purchasing	Imperfections in supplier markets	
Marketing	Imperfections in seller markets	Monopoly policy, tax system

Taxation Induced Distortions

The British tax system *might* have been designed to encourage industrial concentration and the decline of small firms although it was not. It has been built up piece by piece in response to the needs of the day, and political pressures. Tacked on to it are some measures designed to help small firms and at least one feature (the favourable treatment of trading profits under Schedule D) which unintentionally does so, but the overall effect is to distort the structure of economic activity in favour of large units.

Although the trading profits of unincorporated enterprises are, as mentioned, treated somewhat more favourably than those of companies, and there are now reliefs against employment income for start-ups (and numerically most new enterprises are unincorporated) the very nature of taxation is weighted against risk-taking and small business is highly risky. The person who starts his own firm and is successful knows that he will be taxed at progressive rates but if he fails he will get no financial help from the government. There is less asymmetry of this kind in a large firm where losses from a new activity can be offset for tax purposes against profits of an existing activity. As a new small firm grows and the proprietor gets older, the progressivity of the tax system and the fact that capital taxation will eat into anything he can leave for his heirs, act as disincentives to bearing the additional risks and responsibilities of expansion. At the same time the fact that capital gains taxation is lower at the margin than income or corporation taxes gives the small firm proprietor an incentive to sell out to a large firm if he can. The large firm will get tax relief on loans for acquiring another firm but it and its shareholders will be liable for capital gains and dividend taxation if it disposes of its interest in a small subsidiary: another asymmetry which encourages concentration. The motives of small firm proprietors are not only financial in character as we have seen, but it seems likely that tax disincentives must have some unfavourable effect upon both new enterprise and the expansion of existing small enterprises and they have certainly encouraged the acquisition of small firms by large.

Everyone who has tried to fill in his own tax return as an employee knows how complicated the tax system is. Corporate taxation and Schedule D taxation for the self-employed is very much more complicated still. There are some changes in tax regulations every year and professional tax accountants argue endlessly amongst themselves and with the Inland Revenue and Customs and Excise about the interpretation of these regulations. No one can be certain of the tax liability of a small business for any given year until its accounts are finalized and its tax returns agreed with the Revenue. This process typically takes many months after the year end and commonly, where there are changes in legal form, for example, the incorporation of a partnership, it can take several years. Since the skill and knowledge of professional accountants and the financial expertise of proprietors varies, it is highly unlikely that even two closely similar businesses will have exactly the same tax rate. This complexity is itself a discrimination against small firms since they cannot normally afford the best financial advice. Moreover, no one is as assiduous at looking after other people's money as their own. Taxation in its various forms is now so important that no proprietor or director should leave his business tax affairs entirely to his professional advisers. On the other hand if a small businessman concerns himself with taxation, he is diverting his energies away from the growth and expansion of the firm.

Much more important than any of these things, however, is the way the tax system strikes directly at the supply of capital for small firms. Taxes on capital and income make it difficult to accumulate private funds for investment in one's own or other people's business and once a business is making a profit, taxes again slow down the rate at which funds can be saved for investment. At the same time, savings are being channelled by powerful tax incentives into large financial institutions, property and government securities and away from small enterprises.

Even national insurance contributions and the local authority rating system, which are, of course, both part of the tax system, have features which discriminate against small firms. The self-employed are excluded from the graduated state pension scheme and unemployment benefit and yet have to make national insurance contributions at rates which do not fully reflect this discriminating treatment. Employers' national insurance contributions are in effect a tax on labour and thus tend to weigh more heavily on small firms which are labour intensive; they also discriminate against firms employing part-time employees and again small firms make more extensive use of part-time employees than large firms. As to rates, everyone agrees that these are unfair, assessed as they are on a hypothetical and therefore arbitrary basis, but they are also fixed in such a way that local authorities have little or no incentive to promote small business. They make little use of their freedom to provide financial assistance for small firms. Rates are the same whether a firm is prospering or failing and the rate support system so works that a local authority is not necessarily better off if it manages to attract new small firms to set up in its area. Moreover it is probable that rates which bear a rough relation to property values discriminate against small firms for which property costs may be a higher proportion of total costs than for large firms. Finally, a peculiar feature of the rating system is that whilst the owners of businesses pay rates, unless they happen to live in the same local authority area as the one in which their business premises are situated, they are disenfranchised.

In the long run a complete reform of the whole tax system is clearly necessary and possibly an expenditure tax, as proposed by the Meade Committee, may be desirable. However, this would take time and should take time since it is important to get it right. Meanwhile, drastic reform and surgery in the present system is urgently required.

Taxation and Capital Markets

The first step in reform should be to eliminate, as far as possible, capital market distortions arising from differences in the tax treatment of different forms of saving. This would mean abolishing tax relief on insurance premiums, the special treatment of gilt-edged securities and other government savings media and Building Society interest. Action of this kind would have the advantage of broadening the tax base so as to make it possible to reduce basic income tax rates as well as enormously simplifying administration for both the taxpayer and the tax authorities. It would be probably be necessary to withdraw the reliefs in stages if disruption and unfairness were to be minimized. Tax relief on mortgage interest payments also ought to go though this would be unpopular. This relief is being eroded in real terms by inflation (provided the £25,000 limit remains), and would be further eroded by reductions in tax rates. These changes would, in themselves, increase the relative attraction of investment in small business and would, it is hoped, stimulate institutional changes in the capital market in the same direction.

Capital Taxes

Next, capital gains taxation should be integrated with income tax and charged at the same rate after some form

of indexation to eliminate inflationary gains. The revenue
implications of this change are uncertain but some overall
increase in tax revenue could be expected. There is a
theoretical economic justification for charging capital
gains at a lower rate than income: the taxation of capital
can reduce incentives to accumulate it, but the proposed
abolition of corporate taxes would be helpful in this
respect. What the present differential achieves is a
loophole for the wealthy to avoid income tax by converting
income into capital; more important, it also provides a
powerful incentive for small firms to sell out to large
companies. It could be argued that the prospect of a
capital gain also provides a powerful incentive to build a
small company in the first place, but this is simply
unrealistic in the light of what we know about the initial
motivations of most entrepreneurs. The motivations of
third party investors in small firms are, of course, less
ambivalent than those of the owners and it might, for a
time at least, be necessary to give some relief on capital
gains taxation to them. Having got rid of tax
discrimination between different kinds of saving we should
also remove the tax discrimination against investment
income. Like many of the other features of our tax system
which were intended to hit the rich, the investment income
surcharge harms mainly a less favoured group, in this case
elderly people with modest savings that have already been
heavily eroded by inflation. There is no economic
justification for taxing income from savings made out of
income which has already been taxed and it is indefensible
to tax them at a higher rate. The changes proposed to
capital gains tax can be seen as a quid pro quo for the
abolition of the investment income surcharge.

Capital transfer tax is much hated by small firms and its
teeth have, in fact, been progressively pulled. It is doubtful
if it is now a very urgent problem from the wider economic
point of view. There is no evidence that the small firm

population in Britain is suffering from an excessive death rate (particularly a CTT-induced death rate). Our principal concern should be with measures that affect the birth rate of new enterprise. Of course, death duties of any kind are not helpful to small business but they are probably a political inevitability. In the long run it would be better to move towards an inheritance tax in which the recipient, rather than the donor, would be taxed. Such a tax is readily available in (our reformed) capital gains tax.

National Insurance Contributions

National insurance contributions are a more difficult problem; they have more than doubled as a proportion of government revenue since 1955 but are in fact still relatively low in the UK compared with other European countries, though not compared with the US and Japan. However, in Europe there is concern about the adverse effects upon employment of flat-rate or earnings-related social security contributions. One popular suggestion is that employment contributions should be related to value added rather than payroll. That part of the contributions for both employer and employee for earnings-related pensions should probably be left as it is and extended to cover the self-employed. These are at present excluded on the transparently weak argument that variations in income and delays in assessing it make it impractical to assimilate the self-employed. However, other countries manage to overcome these problems and if the self-employed can be taxed they can obviously make graduated pension contributions (both are collected by the Inland Revenue). The rest of national insurance contributions are simply a general tax which might as well be collected by other taxes on income or expenditure and there would be few particular advantages in shifting to a value added base.

Incidentally, the whole system of welfare payments and unemployment benefit could be better integrated into the income tax system so that persons receiving less than a certain minimum income would benefit from 'negative' income tax. This would have the advantage that social security benefits would be assessed for tax. At the moment they are tax free (though this can be expected to change) and in some respects too high in relation to average earnings so that some people have little incentive to work at all.

Corporation Tax

Corporate taxation in Britain is quite absurdly complicated and, for manufacturing companies as a group, performs no useful purpose since its incidence is reduced by investment allowances and stock relief and proceeds are offset by grants and other assistance to companies. Whilst this aid has no identifiably beneficial effect and does some harm in that it delays change and adaptation to market forces, the corporation tax system effectively transfers resources from small to large firms. It is large firms which receive most of the allowances and aid and it is large firms which benefit principally from the corporation tax treatment of loan interest in the acquisition of small firms. Corporation tax also hampers the efforts of small firms to accumulate funds for investment. It is, of course, a relatively efficient tax from the point of view of the Inland Revenue, but it imposes heavy costs and distortions from the viewpoint of the small firm sector. The only other strong reason for retaining corporation tax is that it prevents the avoidance of taxation by building up tax free funds in companies from which shareholders can benefit via the capital gains tax loophole. If capital gains are treated in the same way as income tax then this reason ceases to be valid and corporation tax might as well be abolished altogether. If aids to industry were drastically reduced at the same time, this abolition need have no net adverse effect upon revenue. Capital gains tax for companies should also be abolished. Corporation tax contributes less than 5 per cent of tax revenues and even if budgetary constraints meant that initially abolition would be confined to manufacturing, ultimately it should be extended to all companies. This is important because small firms in service industries must be major contributors to corporation tax revenues. Incidentally the abolition of corporation tax would increase the attractiveness of domestic investment and greatly favour inward investment.

The proposal that taxes on company profit should be abolished will be shocking to those who regard companies in fact, as they are in law, 'persons' (and often wealthy persons) who should not be allowed to 'escape' taxation. In fact, the profits of any company are taxed when they are distributed to the shareholders or drawn as salaries by their owners, so that they cannot escape taxation. If profits are retained and company shares increase in value, capital gains tax is paid on any realizations. Under contemporary conditions there should be no reason to fear that quoted companies would accumulate profits to an excessive degree (it should be remembered that they would be losing government aid) and it would be a good thing for small firms to save for future investment and to see them through bad times. Moreover, it is misleading to think of taxes as necessarily resting where they are levied: it is quite likely that to a large extent, corporation taxes are passed on to consumers. Since the ability of companies to pass taxes forward will be greater in concentrated industries, it is also likely that to the extent that corporation tax is not passed on it bears more heavily on small than large firms.

If corporation tax is to be retained for non-manufacturing companies or in any form there is a strong case for reserving its revenues for local authorities. This would have the advantage (if there were at the same time changes in the rate support grant system) of bringing the interests of local authorities and businesses more in line. However, simpler local corporate taxes – for example, based upon net assets, as in Germany – could be devised to supplement a revised property tax as a substitute for the existing rating system.

Simplification, Reducing Tax Rates and Increasing Tax Yields

These major changes in the tax system would remove many distortions and much discrimination against small firms. They would also greatly simplify things for both the tax-payer and the tax authorities. Careful study would reveal many minor ways in which the complexity of the system could be further reduced. Once this was done it should be practicable for all taxpayers to assess their own tax liability. The present jungle of taxes and tax regulations not only distorts the structure of the economy, it provides enormous scope for avoidance and is extremely inefficient to operate. It would be naive to imagine that taxes can be self-policed, but any tax system which cannot be self-administered and understood by the layman is too complex. Our own system has become a creeping ivy which, if it is not cut back, will continue to stifle enterprise and drive more and more economic activity underground. Although there now seems to be widespread agreement that tax rates have risen to counter-productive levels there is less understanding of the distortions which the system creates. Several European countries, for example Germany, have tax systems which are at least as complicated as ours but they have (or had) lower marginal rates of taxation and in Germany especially, major reliefs and exemptions for small firms. For several reasons, capital market distortions are also less serious in other countries.

It is also important to reduce tax rates, particularly income tax, as well as to simplify the tax system and eliminate its worst distorting effects. Some progress has already been made in this by the Conservative Government which came into power in 1979. Wanting to reduce taxes is not the same as wanting to reduce public expenditure, though it will be necessary to reduce expenditure before tax rates can be brought down and it will take time before the effects of either simplification or reduction come through.

Concentration as a Self-reinforcing Process

Full discussion of the ways in which concentration is self-reinforcing lies outside the scope of a short book. This subject was dealt with at length in *The Juggernauts* (Bannock 1971) but two examples may be given. The growth of large retail chains in the 1950s and 1960s, though a highly desirable and beneficial development in itself, led to an acceleration of mergers in manufacturing industries as the buying power of the multiples made itself felt. Competition amongst suppliers to retail outlets for some classes of goods seems to have become so distorted that there is now price discrimination between large and small retailers. In other words the multiples get lower prices than can be justified by economies in the processing and transport of the large orders they are able to place. Small and even medium-sized shops complain that in some cases goods are sold retail in the multiples at lower than their buying-in prices so that they, and their customers, are subsidizing the larger retailers. It is difficult to get factual information to substantiate these claims. It is perhaps significant that discounts for quantity are not normally published and, of course, information on costs is rarely available, but it seems quite plausible that terms even for large quantities are not the same for all buyers. The Monopolies Commission is investigating this problem now (nine years after such an investigation was recommended by Bolton).

Banking is an example of an industry where concentration in Britain is perhaps greater than in any of the other large industrialized countries. The four major clearing bank groups account for the vast majority of bank deposits and retail branches. The concentration of banking means that control and administration are highly centralized in London and the sheer size of the banks means that their operations are highly bureaucratized, though very efficient: as retail groups, the British clearers are the best in the world. Since small business is essentially a local activity, there can be little doubt that whatever other advantages have been gained from concentration in banking, services to small firms as a group have suffered. Recent developments in the banking system, for example the separation of corporate from other customer services, attempts to give branch managers more discretion and so on, are a recognition of the problems of centralized banking. It is not difficult to imagine that a system of local banks each with their own staff permanently located in the area, collecting savings locally and lending locally, would be more flexible and more sensitive to local needs than the present system. This was the system which existed 50 years ago. In fact, the banking system, or parts of it, in many other countries is still much more like this than it is in Britain where even Saturday morning opening is barred by tacit agreement amongst the banks (and their staff unions). The Building Societies, which are to some extent locally based, are not allowed by law to lend to private business.

More generally, as industry has become more concentrated, what J. K. Galbraith calls 'bureaucratic symbiosis' has moved it closer to government so that the supervisory agencies and departments have become pressure groups serving the interests of the large companies that they are supposed to be regulating. The political power of large companies and the trades unions, which in this respect have mutually fostered each other, is the ultimate reason why the social and economic system has been progressively biased against the interests of small firms. This has not been a conspiracy, nor has it been intentional, but in the absence of strong counter-pressure from small firm interests and a lack of understanding of the issues in successive governments, it is not surprising that these interests have suffered.

Monopolies and Merger Policy

Any serious policy to reverse the process of concentration must include measures to control monopolies, and in particular to discourage all large mergers. Mergers are the major cause of increasing concentration, yet even existing powers to control them are little used. Between 1965 and 1973 the Mergers Panel examined 800 mergers involving the acquisition of gross assets exceeding £5 million or where the market share of the parties involved exceeded one third. Only twenty of these were referred to the Monopolies Commission and only six were prohibited (though a further seven were abandoned voluntarily). The difficulty is that, as Hannah and Kay (1977) point out, while it cannot usually be argued convincingly in each individual case that the merger is against the public interest, an indefinite continuation of mergers and concentration cannot be in the public interest. At least until enough new enterprises are being formed and growing up to challenge existing market leaders, then it would be better to prohibit all mergers involving substantial assets and firms with statutory monopoly (now a market share of 25 per cent or more). Machinery would probably have to allow for appeal in particular cases, but the criteria upon which a major merger could be in the public interest should be severely limiting, for example to cases where planned rationalizations of capacity or mainly overseas activities were involved. The assessment of the public interest is, as experience in the Monopolies Commission has shown, exceptionally difficult and simply because of this, if larger mergers were banned outright it is doubtful that much would be lost.

Once concentration has taken place it is much more difficult to control the consequences by regulatory action: this is why the need to control mergers is so urgent. The use of an investigatory body (the Monopolies Commission) with powers to prohibit action of the kind now embodied in UK legislation is not necessarily superior to the more judicial approach in the United States, but it is essential that the Commission should be given closer guidance upon how the public interest is to be assessed.

Changes in taxation should have a powerful reversing effect upon concentration and a tougher merger policy should help arrest further increases. The effects of changes which have come about over a half century and more will take a long time to unravel, and powerful vested interests have built up which will not easily be dislodged. Other measures therefore will be necessary.

Finance and Company Law

Some positive discrimination in favour of small firms is necessary in two areas: finance and company law. A government backed credit guarantee scheme, probably operated through the commercial banks, would help to increase lending, particularly where this is held up through lack of acceptable security. More should also be done to lower the cost of finance for small firms: this means subsidized lending schemes, some of which, at least, should be directed at the equity problem for start-ups and very small firms. Details of measures of this kind are outside the scope of this book, but so much has been learned about them over a very long period in other countries that it should not be impossible to devise workable and effective methods. The cost would be trivial in relation to the social benefits. As little as £500 million or about 0.07 per cent of total public expenditure might be adequate. The case for measures of these kinds is rapidly gaining acceptance but it may take some time before anything is done.

In company law and other legislation affecting business some bold and imaginative measures are necessary, particularly since little can be learned from abroad. Virtually all contemporary legislation is drafted with large firms in mind with only minor concessions to the different needs and problems of small firms. What is needed is entirely new legislation for very small companies of the proprietary type that would provide a simple and complete 'package' of rules and regulations, simpler taxation and which would also exempt them from other provisions of specified legislation. Thus small firms registering as a proprietary business (the distinction between company and sole trader or partnership could possibly be abandoned along with corporation tax) would be exempt from the provisions of the Companies Act, the Employment Protection Act, consumer protection laws and so on, but would be bound by such elements in these other pieces of legislation as were seen fit to be reincorporated in the new law. The provisions of this new law should be set out in a booklet of less than a dozen pages. Limited liability, as now, should involve more onerous registration qualifications but within the same framework. All proprietary companies would be ineligible for registration for VAT and it would be intended to apply to quite small enterprises only, those with a turnover of less than £50,000 or five employees. Such businesses should be able to opt for imputed income by the tax authorities which would vary according to trade. These measures should slow the growth of the Black Economy.

This is a very different proposal from that made at the end of the 1960s by the accounting bodies for Proprietary Company legislation. This was intended to include much larger independent owner-managed companies with up to 200 employees, that is to say, most private companies, and to distinguish them from public (including quoted) companies and larger private companies which are not effectively managed by their owners and which were to be described as stewardship companies. The objectives of these proposals were primarily to relieve smaller private companies of the increasingly complex requirements for the disclosure of accounting and other information. The Bolton Committee recommended that this proposal should be seriously considered in revising company law, but it has not so far been adopted, presumably on the grounds of fears about administrative difficulties which might arise. These objections would be met by our proposals for a separate legal category for tiny firms where it is possible to go much further in simplifying administrative requirements for both government and industry. It is estimated that over 40 per cent of private businesses would qualify for our proposals. The problems of small private companies with between 5 and 200 employees could and should be met by more generous exemptions from disclosure and other legal requirements.

Scope for Other Government Action

Much more needs to be done by government to remove discrimination against small firms and avoid the damaging economic consequences that flow from it. In some instances, for example in paperwork and attitudes to planning applications from small firms in urban areas, there has recently been some improvement, but there remain vast areas of government responsibilities which do not yet reflect any sensitivity at all to the problem of small firms, let alone the magnitude of the problem. In the long run the decentralization of government (which is necessary and probably inevitable for other reasons) will also be required, but much could be done within the existing structure.

The educational system, for example, is heavily biased against training for the artisans that are so essential to the emergence of small firms in, for example, the engineering and construction industries and in favour of non-manual skills. The root of this bias is presumably the belief that contemporary technological and economic development is primarily service based and requires rapidly diminishing inputs of skilled manual labour. That this is not so is patently obvious from a study of West Germany, a more advanced economy than our own. There, over 4 million persons are employed in the half million or so small enterprises classified as Handwerk, 168,000 firms in metal working industries alone – more than double the *total* number of firms of all sizes in British manufacturing industry.

Another 'blind' area in the public sector is public purchasing which continues, as far as it is possible to tell, to be overwhelmingly concentrated on large firms. The regulation of the banking system also does nothing to facilitate lending to small firms. There is no reason why Building Societies, for example, should not be encouraged to provide finance for small business premises, and possibly the Trustee Savings Banks could play a role in the provision of finance for small firms.

A New Institution

It is very desirable that the political will, which now exists to promote small enterprises in Britain, should be reinforced and nourished by a new institution which can articulate the needs of the sector, that is, voice its vested interests, speak out against the vested interests of others, monitor the effects of government action on small firms, carry out research and develop practical solutions to policy problems. In the United States, these functions are combined with the administration of Federal programmes to assist small business in an independent and public agency, the Small Business Administration. It is doubtful if such an agency is the right solution in Britain and the continental approach of a Ministry for Middle Classes is also inappropriate, requiring as it does the back-up of powerful interest groups which do not exist in this country. The real gap is not in the administration of programmes — the Civil Service is capable enough of doing that — but in research, advocacy and criticism. Left to itself the government service is all too likely to come up with more and more special tax reliefs (which would complicate the tax system still further), specific support schemes for industry (the latest vogue is for New Technology Based Firms) and other paternalistic and interventionist devices which are not what small business requires and which, as applied to large firms, are to a large extent responsible for the problem we now face.

Research, advocacy and criticism ought to be supplied by the small firm representative bodies themselves, and already is to a limited extent. Although much stronger than they were ten years ago, these bodies are still weak and fragmented, but it might be possible to persuade the strongest among them (only one has more than a few thousand direct members and none is in any sense fully representative of small firms) to join an advisory council with a strong secretariat partly financed by public funds.

Action by Small and Large Firms

It is not intended to suggest that action is required only by government. Probably the most effective thing that small firm proprietors can do is to join a small firm organization and give some of their valuable time to make sure that it is effective. They can also try hard to stand back from the daily battle and ask themselves if they are as open to modern developments and opportunities as they should be. We must not romanticize about small firms: many are backward and reluctant to change. They survive only because their proprietors are willing to accept less than the market rate for their own services. It certainly is true that the incidence of industrial action (strikes) is directly related to size of establishment. This is partly the result of the difficulties of communication between management and employee, but it probably mainly reflects the lower degree of unionization in small and medium-sized firms. Sociologists have devoted little attention to industrial relationships in small firms, but recent work by Stanworth and Curran suggests that employees do not necessarily choose to work in small firms because they expect working conditions to be happier. Some small firm proprietors are rogues, they evade taxes, they are ruthless employers and they short-change their customers. This is only human nature and does not provide justification for throttling the honest majority with rules and regulations.

Large firms, too, can help. One of the most heartening

features of the recent shift in favour of small firms is that some large firms are now taking positive action to help small business. The Work of Shell, the Midland and Barclays Banks, ICFC, BP, BOC, IBM and Marks and Spencers in the London Enterprise Agency is a case in point, but ICI, Pilkingtons and others have also acted independently. This phenomenon seems to be mainly confined to Britain and the United States, but it suggests that large firms are now beginning to realize that their own interests and those of small firms are indivisible.

The broad outlines of new policies for small firms sketched out here will sound very radical to many people, but ten years ago they could not even have been put forward seriously. There are many encouraging signs that some of the myths influencing established opinion about industrial organization are breaking down and small business, which has been out in the wilderness for many decades, is now coming back into the mainstream of public policy. It is to be hoped that it will do so not in the 'Small is Beautiful' sense of an escape from, or an alternative to, the problems of growth and affluence, but as an essential part of the industrial and post-industrial economy: in other words as part of the reality of the modern world.

SELECT BIBLIOGRAPHY

Binks, M. 1979: Finance for Expansion in the Small Firm, *Lloyds Bank Review*, October.

Bolton, J. E. 1971: *Small Firms, Report of the Committee of Inquiry on Small Firms*, HMSO.

Bannock, G. 1971: *The Juggernauts*, Weidenfeld and Nicolson.

1975: *How to Survive the Slump*, Penguin Books.

1976: *Smaller Business in Britain and Germany*, Wilton House Publications.

1980: *The Organisation of Public Sector Promotion of Small Business*, Economists Advisory Group for Shell UK Ltd.

Bannock G. and Doran, A. 1978: *Small Firms in Cities*, Economists Advisory Group for Shell UK, Ltd.

Birch, D. L. 1979: *The Job Generation Process*, Massachusetts Institute of Technology, mimeo.

Fothergill, S. and Gudgin, G. 1979: *The Job Generation Process in Britain*, Centre for Environmental Studies Research Series No 32, November.

Galbraith, J. K. 1967: *The New Industrial Estate*, Hamish Hamilton.

Gudgin, G., Brunskill, I. and Fothergill, S. 1979: *New Manufacturing Firms in Regional Employment Growth*, Centre for Environmental Studies Research Series, October.

Hannah, L. and Kay, J. A. 1977: *Concentration in Modern Industry*, Macmillan.

Institute of Bankers 1978: *The Banks and Small Business*, Institute of Bankers.

Jewkes, J., Sawers, D., and Stillerman, R. 1969: *The Sources of Invention*, Macmillan.

Prais, S. J. 1976: *The Evolution of Giant Firms in Britain*, Cambridge University Press.

Schumacher, E. F. 1973: *Small is Beautiful*, Blond and Briggs.

Schumpeter, J. A. 1943: *Capitalism, Socialism and Democracy*, Allen and Unwin.

Servan-Schrieber, J. J. 1968: *The American Challenge*, Hamish Hamilton.

Wilson, H. 1979: *The Financing of Small Firms. Interim Report of the Committee to Review the Functioning of Financial Institutions*, HMSO.

World Bank 1978: *Employment and Development of Small Enterprises*, World Bank, Washington.

Index